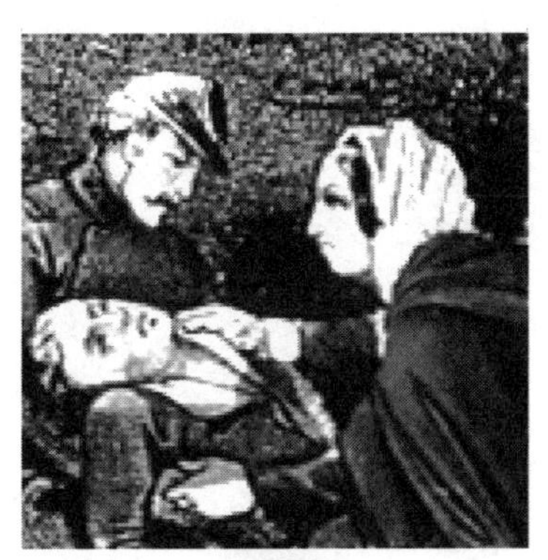

AN UNFINISHED BATTLE

AMERICAN WOMEN 1848-1865

THE YOUNG OXFORD HISTORY OF WOMEN IN THE UNITED STATES

Nancy F. Cott, *General Editor*

AN UNFINISHED BATTLE

AMERICAN WOMEN 1848-1865

Harriet Sigerman

OXFORD UNIVERSITY PRESS

New York • Oxford

To my father, Leon Sigerman, and in loving memory of my mother, Lillian Sophie Sigerman

Oxford University Press

Oxford New York Toronto
Delhi Bombay Calcutta Madras Karachi
Kuala Lumpur Singapore Hong Kong Tokyo
Nairobi Dar es Salaam Cape Town
Melbourne Auckland Madrid

and associated companies in
Berlin Ibadan

Published by Oxford University Press, Inc., 200 Madison Avenue, New York, New York 10016

Oxford is a registered trademark of Oxford University Press, Inc.

Library of Congress Cataloging-in-Publication Data

Sigerman, Harriet.
An unfinished battle: American women, 1848-1865 / Harriet Sigerman.
p. cm. — (The Young Oxford history of women in the United States ; v. 5)
Includes bibliographical references and index.
ISBN 0-19-508110-2
ISBN 0-19-508830-1 (series)
1. Women—United States—History—19th century—Juvenile literature. 2. Women—United States—Social conditions—Juvenile literature. [1. Women—History—19th century. 2. Women—Social conditions—19th century. 3. United States—Social conditions—19th century.]
I. Title II. Series.
HQ1418.S57 1994
305.4'0973'09034—dc20 93-34874
CIP
AC

1 3 5 7 9 8 6 4 2

Printed in the United States of America
on acid-free paper

Design: Leonard Levitsky
Layout: Loraine Machlin
Picture Research: Lisa Kirchner, Laura Kreiss

On the Cover: The Night after the Battle, lithograph by Currier & Ives, 1863.
Frontispiece: The organizers of the New York Sanitary Fair of 1864, which raised more than $1 million for aid to Union soldiers.

CONTENTS

INTRODUCTION

The year 1848 was a year of revolution in Europe. The German philosopher Karl Marx published *The Communist Manifesto;* the British philosopher John Stuart Mill published *The Principles of Political Economy;* and a small number of socialist women in France demanded their own political rights in the midst of an uprising that overthrew the French monarchy. The same year, several determined women in upstate New York called a convention, attended by almost 300 women and men, that drew up a declaration modeled on the 1776 Declaration of Independence. The 1848 declaration detailed the many wrongs of gender inequality rather than those of colonial government. The Declaration of Sentiments made at Seneca Falls marked the formal beginning of the women's rights movement in the United States.

The year 1848 ushered in the tumultuous middle years of the 19th century—years of increasing political activism by women's groups, antislavery agitators, and supporters of slavery. These years also saw the geographical expansion of white settlement across a continent, the annexation of formerly Spanish and Mexican territory, the discovery of gold in California, the growth of cities and industries in the Northeast, the extension of "king cotton" and the grip of racial slavery to the near Southwest, and the development of sectional interests in the nation so bitterly different that they would result in

During the Civil War some black and white women worked together to cook meals and care for wounded soldiers. This rare photograph was taken in a hospital tent in Virginia.

the catastrophe of the Civil War. How women participated in all of these events forms the story of this book. The voices of women—pioneers and displaced Native Americans, slaves and slaveholders, industrial wage earners and the wives and daughters of capitalist entrepreneurs, political radicals and demure conservatives, women who served the Union in the Civil War and the Confederacy—sound through these pages.

This book is part of a series that covers the history of women in the United States from the 17th through 20th century. Traditional historical writing has dealt almost entirely with men's lives because men have, until very recently, been the heads of state, the political officials, judges, ministers, and business leaders who have wielded the most visible and recorded power. But for several recent decades, new interest has arisen in social and cultural history, where common people are the actors who create trends and mark change as well as continuity. An outpouring of research and writing on women's history has been part of this trend to look at individuals and groups who have not held the reins of rule in their own hands but nonetheless participated in making history. The motive to address and correct sexual inequality in society has also vitally influenced women's history, on the thinking that knowledge of the past is essential to creating justice for the future.

The histories in this series look at many aspects of women's lives. The books ask new questions about the course of American history. How did the type and size of families change, and what difference did that make in people's lives? What expectations for women differed from those for men, and how did such expectations change over the centuries? What roles did women play in the economy? What form did women's political participation take when they could not vote? And how did politics change when women did gain full citizenship? How did women work with other women who were like or unlike them, as well as with men, for social and political goals? What sex-specific constraints or opportunities did they face? The series aims to understand the diverse women who have peopled American history by investigating their work and leisure, family patterns, political activities, forms of organization, and outstanding accomplishments. Standard events of American history, from the settling of the continent to the American Revolution, the Civil War, industrialization, American entry onto the world stage, and world wars, are all here, too, but seen from the point of view of women's experiences. Together, the answers to new questions and the treatment of old ones from women's points of view make up a compelling narrative of four centuries of history in the United States.

—Nancy F. Cott

VOLUME 1
The Tried and the True
Native American Women Confronting Colonization

VOLUME 2
The Colonial Mosaic
American Women 1600-1760

VOLUME 3
The Limits of Independence
American Women 1760-1800

VOLUME 4
Breaking New Ground
American Women 1800-1848

VOLUME 5
An Unfinished Battle
American Women 1848-1865

VOLUME 6
Laborers for Liberty
American Women 1865-1890

VOLUME 7
New Paths to Power
American Women 1890-1920

VOLUME 8
From Ballots to Breadlines
American Women 1920-1940

VOLUME 9
Pushing the Limits
American Women 1940-1961

VOLUME 10
The Road to Equality
American Women Since 1962

VOLUME 11
Supplement and Index

"I HAD MUCH RATHER STARVE THAN BE A SLAVE"

On December 21, 1848, a slight young man and his strapping slave boarded the steamer *General Clinch* in Savannah, Georgia, for a trip to Charleston, South Carolina. The young man seemed to be ailing. He was bundled up in a large overcoat, and his face—or, rather, what was left uncovered by an enormous pair of spectacles—was swathed in a white handkerchief, like a bandage. He acted self-conscious, eager to avoid attention. Perhaps he felt embarrassed by his frail condition. He introduced himself to the ship's steward as Mr. Johnson and asked to be shown to his berth so that he could rest.

The next morning, he made his appearance, still dressed in the same clothes as the night before. As his fellow passengers glanced over at him, he quietly took a seat. One of the other passengers, curious about him, questioned the man's slave. The slave explained that Mr. Johnson was an invalid who was afflicted with rheumatism and was barely able to walk. He and the slave were on their way to Philadelphia, to consult Mr. Johnson's uncle, a well-known physician. Mr. Johnson hoped that his uncle could cure his disease. After hearing this sad tale, the passenger felt mildly sympathetic toward Mr. Johnson, though he thought it strange that Mr. Johnson walked so spryly for a person plagued by rheumatism.

Upon arriving in Charleston, Mr. Johnson and his slave hailed a carriage and instructed the driver to take them to the best hotel in

Bondage drove many slaves to acts of desperation, and suicide was the only answer for many of them.

Ellen Craft disguised herself as a man to make her escape, a feat that made international news. This illustration of her disguise was printed in the Illustrated London News.

town. As their carriage pulled up, the hotel keeper came out to greet them. When he saw how ill Mr. Johnson was, all bundled up and holding two warm poultices against his cheeks, the hotel keeper took him very gently by the arm and ordered a servant to take his other arm. Together, they carefully led Mr. Johnson inside.

Mr. Johnson asked for a bedroom, and the hotel keeper told his servant to take him to a comfortable room. Together, the servant and Mr. Johnson's slave helped him into the room, and the slave ordered two more hot poultices for his master. Mr. Johnson rested from his voyage, and the next day, he and his slave left Charleston and boarded another steamer bound for Wilmington, North Carolina. From Wilmington, they journeyed to Baltimore, the last slaveholding city on their route, to catch a train for Philadelphia.

In Baltimore, the railroad agent informed Mr. Johnson that he would have to show proof of ownership of his slave. He explained that runaway slaves often used Baltimore as an escape point into Pennsylvania, a free state. Mr. Johnson seemed troubled by this news. He grew indignant when the agent asked to see his ownership papers. He explained that he had neglected to bring any proof of ownership. When the agent asked if any "gentleman" in Baltimore could attest to his ownership, he replied, greatly vexed, "I bought tickets in Charleston to pass us through to Philadelphia, and therefore you have no right to detain us here."

"Well, sir," the officer replied, growing annoyed himself, "right or no right, we shan't let you go."

By now, their loud voices had drawn the attention of other passengers, who seemed to take pity on Mr. Johnson. They hissed at the insensitive agent for giving this poor gentleman such a hard time. The bell clanged to announce the train was departing, and every eye turned to Mr. Johnson and the agent, who by now was thoroughly confused as to what to do. Scratching his head, he said, "I calculate it is all right." Then he turned and instructed a clerk to tell the conductor that Mr. Johnson and his slave would be allowed to board. Referring to Mr. Johnson, he said, "As he is not well, it is a pity to stop him here. We will let him go."

After this trying delay, Mr. Johnson and his slave completed the last leg of their journey. On Christmas morning, 1848, their train pulled into Philadelphia. They would have a joyous Christmas after all—and not simply because they had finally arrived at their destination. Mr. Johnson and his slave had just pulled off one of the most ingenious escapades ever attempted by two runaway slaves. Mr. Johnson, as it turned out, was not really an ailing young slaveholder, nor did his "slave" belong to him. Instead, Mr. Johnson was Ellen Craft, a slave woman who had escaped from a plantation in Macon, Georgia, along with her husband, William, who played the role of her slave.

In the weeks leading up to their escape, they had devised this clever plan. They carefully tried to conceal any indication that Ellen was a woman. Because she had no beard, they cooked up the story that she was ailing and was forced to wear a scarf holding two poultices to conceal her face. And because she did not know how to write, and therefore would not be able to sign her name in a hotel register, they decided to put her arm in a fake sling, as if she were temporarily unable to use a pen.

Freedom obviously meant a great deal for Ellen and William Craft to contrive such an elaborate plan. Ellen was the daughter of a white master and an enslaved mother. She had been given to her master's daughter as a wedding present. She was a favored servant, and so her life as a slave had not been as harsh as that of other slaves. William, who was also a slave, had been hired out by his master to a cabinetmaker and was also allowed to moonlight as a hotel waiter to earn a little extra money. After months of saving, he had scraped up enough money to finance their escape.

Although neither slave had experienced the worst hardships of bondage, both were desperate to escape from slavery—especially Ellen, who had been sold away from her mother as a child and who feared that any children she bore could be sold away from her. She and William had planned their escape carefully, and it went off without a hitch except for the problem of the papers in Baltimore.

In Philadelphia, the couple took refuge with a Quaker family for a few days, then journeyed to New England. By now, news of their ingenious escape had spread, but they were safe in New England until 1850. That year, Congress passed the Fugitive Slave Law, which gave southern slaveowners more power than any previous law to arrest runaway slaves in the North and return them to slavery. Like other runaways, Ellen and William Craft were at risk of

CAUTION!!

COLORED PEOPLE

OF BOSTON, ONE & ALL,

You are hereby respectfully CAUTIONED and advised, to avoid conversing with the

Watchmen and Police Officers of Boston,

For since the recent ORDER OF THE MAYOR & ALDERMEN, they are empowered to act as

KIDNAPPERS

AND

Slave Catchers,

And they have already been actually employed in KIDNAPPING, CATCHING, AND KEEPING SLAVES. Therefore, if you value your LIBERTY, and the *Welfare of the Fugitives* among you, *Shun* them in every possible manner, as so many *HOUNDS* on the track of the most unfortunate of your race.

Keep a Sharp Look Out for KIDNAPPERS, and have TOP EYE open.

APRIL 24, 1851.

Black people in the North lived under the constant threat of capture by zealous government officials and bounty hunters. Rigid enforcement of the Fugitive Slave Law was a threat not only to escaped slaves but also to the people who sheltered them.

This proslavery cartoon, portraying happy slaves dancing the night away, was published in Boston in 1850. Not all Northerners were abolitionists.

being seized and brought back to the South. When two agents of their former masters appeared in Boston, antislavery workers helped the Crafts escape once more, and they made their way to Maine, and then to Nova Scotia, Canada. From there, they sailed for England, safe from the clutches of their former owners. In England, they went to school to learn how to read and write and taught their fellow students manual skills such as carpentry. They also published an account of their famous escape, entitled *Running a Thousand Miles for Freedom.*

Somehow, a rumor started circulating back in the States that Ellen wished to return to her master in Georgia. She quickly quashed the rumor. "God forbid that I should ever be so false to liberty as to prefer slavery in its stead," she wrote to the *Liberator*, a well-known antislavery journal in the United States. "I had much rather starve in England, a free woman, than be a slave for the best man that ever breathed upon the American continent."

After the Civil War, the Crafts returned to the United States and used their savings to purchase a plantation in Georgia. They also opened an industrial school for former slaves.

With daring, careful planning, and sheer luck, the Crafts had succeeded in reaching the promised land of freedom. Other slaves who tried to escape were less lucky: They died trying or were captured and returned to bondage—often after suffering severe punishment for their attempt to escape. They remained enslaved, toiling for someone who owned their very birthright and who could force them to marry against their will or separate them from loved ones and sell them away.

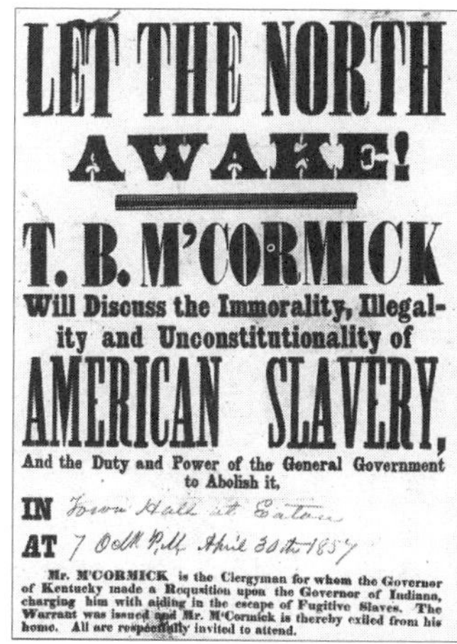

This 1857 poster announces a speech by T. B. McCormick in Eaton, Ohio, about the evils of slavery. McCormick had helped slaves escape from his native Kentucky and was now himself a fugitive from justice.

But the impact of slavery echoed far beyond the fate of the individual slave. In the years leading up to the Civil War, the entire nation was swept up in a fiery debate over slavery. What would be the future of this "peculiar institution," as Abraham Lincoln called it? Should it be allowed to flourish and spread into new territories, as slaveholders wanted, or be abolished, as a growing number of Northerners demanded? As the debate raged and civil war loomed closer, black and white women added their voices to the turmoil—as slaves and mistresses, antislavery workers, and crusaders for their own rights. These were trying, tumultuous years for Americans who wrestled with the moral problems of slavery and sexual inequality in a society that claimed to live by the principles of freedom and fairness for all.

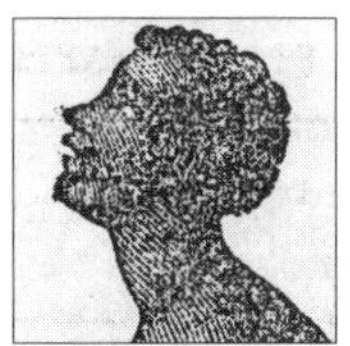

CHAPTER 1

"THOSE AWFUL DAYS": WOMEN IN BONDAGE

Slavery came to the New World almost as soon as the first colonists set foot on American soil. The first black slaves arrived, mainly from the west coast of Africa, during the 17th century. They were imported by British slave traders and later by American colonists. Although slavery had died out or was abolished in the North by the mid-1820s, it continued to thrive in the South. Cotton, the chief economic export of the South, depended upon slave labor. Slaves also planted and harvested other important cash crops, including tobacco, sugar, hemp, rice, and corn.

Most Southerners were poor to middling farmers or workers. But a small number of wealthy plantation owners wielded considerable economic and political power within southern society. They jealously protected the institution of slavery because of the profits they reaped from the unpaid labor of their human property—their slaves.

This image of a woman who has unsuccessfully begged her master not to separate her from her children appeared in the Liberty Almanac *for 1852. The original caption reads, "What can she do? She can only direct her weeping eye to the God of the oppressed, and cry, 'How long wilt thou forget me, O Lord? forever?'"*

Slave children, both boys and girls, grew up in a community in which they were cared for by many adults, including their white mistresses. They spent precious little time with their own parents. Sometimes a mother or father had been sold to another plantation, or an enslaved child was sold away from his or her parents. Even when parents and children lived on the same plantation, both parents worked such long days either in the fields or in the big house—

Men, women, and children work together to bring in the cotton they have picked on a plantation near Vicksburg, Mississippi. The scene was captured by artist William Henry Brown in 1842.

the house where the planter and his family lived—that they had little time left to spend with their own children.

Slave girls seldom enjoyed a carefree childhood. Often they were given chores to do at an earlier age than slave boys. By the age of four or five, they were expected to help care for the planter's children or do small chores around the big house. At six, a young slave girl might be taken into the big house to learn to cook and clean.

One former slave later described the full day's work she put in as a six-year-old child. Although she said she "didn't have to work very hard," she had to get up "way before daylight" to light the fire in the kitchen. Then she had to tote in fresh water from a nearby spring, return to get the container of milk that had been cooling there for the night, and do other chores before breakfast was ready. When the master and mistress sat down to eat, "I stand behind them and shoo off the flies."

Another woman recalled that at age nine she had to make all of the beds in the big house, clean the house, and do other chores such as lowering the shades at night, filling every water pitcher, and arranging all the towels on the washstands. "We wasn't 'lowed to sit down. We had to be doing something all day. Whenebber we was in de presence of any of de white folks, we had to stand up."

When children did not perform their chores correctly or snatched a biscuit or piece of fruit from the pantry because they were hungry, they were punished severely. Either the planter, the mistress, or the overseer, an official hired by the master to supervise the slaves, administered the punishment. One five-year-old girl was forced to swallow worms as punishment for not picking all of the worms off the tobacco leaves. Other children received brutal whippings for minor offenses.

Perhaps more cruel than the physical punishment was being sold away from parents and brothers and sisters to other plantations, sometimes just down the road, and other times many miles away. One ex-slave recalled the tragic day in 1860 when she was sold away. She never even had a chance to hug or kiss her parents good-bye. Her owner and two slave buyers snatched her while her parents were off working in the fields. As she later told an interviewer, who wrote her words down exactly as she said them in southern black dialect, "Me hollerin' at de top o' my voice an' callin' my Ma! Den dem [slave buyers] begin to sing loud—jes to drown out my hollerin'." She never saw her parents again.

Some slave children were more fortunate. Perhaps they belonged to masters who believed in keeping slave families together and would not sell off family members. Some masters treated their slaves with care and consideration. They provided adequate food and clothing, and did not beat them.

By the age of 10, a female slave was considered a half-hand, and she began to work even longer and harder each day. Girls and boys no longer wore the same simple smocklike shirts. The girls wore dresses, usually made out of coarse cotton homespun or calico, and the boys wore rough-cut trousers. Girls began to work more closely with adult female slaves, and became more keenly aware of the different ways that men and women worked, dressed, and were expected to behave. Perhaps more important, they became fully aware of the power that whites had over their lives.

An entire family—mother, father, and child—goes on the block at a Virginia slave auction. Enslaved parents and children lived under the constant fear of being sold away from each other.

Slave women assigned to field work often had no choice but to take along their children. They either carried them in cloth backpacks or laid them in the shade of a tree. Motherhood did not exempt them from the overseer's cruelty.

By puberty, around age 13 or 14, the young slave girl was doing the work of an adult female slave. For most young people, puberty is a rite of passage into a stage between childhood and adulthood. For enslaved children of both sexes, puberty marked the unfortunate rite of passage into full bondage, and teenage slaves were forced to work as hard as their parents.

Women fully shared in the hard physical labor, and they put in workdays that often lasted from before sunup to way past dark or whenever the last of the chores was finished. "I had to do everythin' dey was to do on de outside," recalled a former female slave. "Work in de field, chop wood, hoe corn, till sometime I feels like my back surely break." Female slaves helped to build bridges, plow fields, split rails, and make bricks. "I have done ever thing on a farm what a man done 'cept cut wheat," boasted another ex-slave. Female slaves also worked in cotton and woolen mills, sugar refineries, and mines and foundries. Here, too, the workday was long and grueling—usually 12 to 16 hours, six days a week.

The master's son on a Louisiana plantation sat for a daguerreotype portrait with his "mammy." The relationships between children and the slaves who raised them were often close and long-lasting.

Although female slaves performed the same hard labor as male slaves, there were certain tasks that only women did. These included doing laundry, spinning, weaving, and sewing. Women also developed special skills. For example, slave women who were well versed in roots and bark knew how to make special dyes for coloring clothes. Some women turned their knowledge of herbs, often passed down from mother to daughter, to good use by creating homemade remedies for both the planter's family and the slave community. They made tea from the bark of a gum tree to ease menstrual cramps and treated whooping cough, diarrhea, toothaches, colds, fevers, headaches, and backaches with broths made from tree leaves, bark, twigs, or branches.

After a violent slave revolt in Virginia in 1831, slavery became even more harsh. Slaves could no longer leave their owners' plantations without special permission and passes; if they were caught without the required pass, punishment was swift, usually a whipping. Even a slave husband visiting his wife on another plantation was punished if caught without a pass. In Mississippi, slaves were prohibited from beating drums or blowing horns for fear they were signaling to revolt. And throughout the South, slaves could not carry guns or other weapons, gather in large groups without permission of their masters, or learn to read and write—though some owners taught their slaves, and a few slaves even attended schools with their masters' permission.

But other slaves risked punishment for getting an education. Susie King Taylor, born a slave in 1848 in Georgia, was taught to read and write by a free black woman. One by one, the slave students would enter her house, their books wrapped in paper, so that whites would think they were learning a trade instead of going to school.

Female slaves helped sustain one another during the awful years of bondage. Women slaves often spent the day together, at work and during meal breaks. As they worked, they shared moments by singing work songs and swapping stories about the long workday. They even looked forward to certain tasks, such as doing laundry, because they could visit together while they worked. Quiltings, or "frolics" and "parties," as some female slaves called them, were a special time—a time to be together.

On rural plantations, doing the laundry was a backbreaking task done outdoors by slave women. On this plantation, the women at least had each other's company as they worked. Friendships among African-American women helped to ease the many hardships of slavery, especially when they could share the toil.

Together and alone, slave women and men found ways to defy planters and lessen the hardships of bondage. The most obvious form of resistance—and also the most dangerous because capture brought swift punishment and sometimes death—was escape. Slaves escaped alone or in groups, and ex-slaves helped their enslaved brethren escape. Harriet Tubman, a brave, daring woman who stood only five feet tall, was a field slave in Maryland until she escaped to the North in 1849. But after securing her freedom, this courageous woman returned to the slaveholding states 19 times to rescue other slaves. Risking her own liberty and her life, she helped more than 300 slaves

During the Civil War, the fearless Harriet Tubman (far left), legendary conductor of the Underground Railroad, worked among former slaves as a nurse and teacher. On the Sea Islands, off Georgia, she taught the freedwomen how to launder Union soldiers' uniforms for pay.

reach freedom. Tubman quickly earned the nickname "Moses" after the biblical Moses, who led the ancient Hebrews out of slavery and into the Promised Land.

Using forged passes and sometimes dressing in disguise—once as a farmer setting out for market carrying two chickens by the feet—Tubman usually made her trips during winter because the nights were longer. She led slaves at night through the woods and along backroads, and hid them during the day in swamps, barns, and the homes of antislavery citizens who lived along the Underground Railroad, a secret network of escape routes to the North. Tubman never lost a slave during her daring escapes—but she came close one night. She and 25 runaways had hidden in a swamp all day and night. One of the male slaves became frightened and wanted to turn back. Tubman whipped out a revolver, pointed it at his head, and warned, "Move or die!" He did not turn back and, along with the others, made his way to freedom.

Slaves escaped however they could. Like the ingenious Ellen and William Craft, they devised clever ways to elude slave catchers. Lear Green had herself shipped to Philadelphia in a sailor's chest, and Maria Weems disguised herself as a young boy. Work songs and spirituals sung by slaves in the fields or at their religious gatherings often concealed a message unbeknownst to white owners—instructions on how to find the Underground Railroad. "The river bank will make a very good road/The dead trees show you the way," went one song. "Left foot, peg foot traveling on/Following the drinking gourd." In this song, "peg foot" referred to an old white man with a wooden leg who guided escapees North, and the "drinking gourd" referred to the Big Dipper, the constellation in the sky that signified the direction North.

Slave men and women who did not escape resisted in other ways. Some fought back when planters or overseers beat them. Mary Armstrong almost blinded her mistress with a rock when she tried to whip her. Other slaves took the cowhide right out of their masters' or mistresses' hands and thrashed them instead. A few tried to kill their owners by poisoning them or setting barns or houses on fire. But such drastic measures were risky because if a slave failed, he or she faced certain death in order to serve as a lesson to other slaves contemplating a similar idea.

Some slave women could not abide the idea of bringing enslaved children into the world. With the help of a sympathetic midwife, pregnant women found ways to induce abortions. If they did not have abortions, some women resorted to killing their newborn infants rather than give the planter more slaves.

In less dramatic ways as well, slave women and men resisted their owners—by doing tasks only halfway or by "accidentally on purpose" breaking a mistress's cherished vase while dusting in the big house. Some slaves also pretended to be ill and unable to work—though eagle-eyed owners and overseers caught on to that trick quickly—and others pretended not to hear a master's instructions. If they were house servants, slaves got back at their owners by making off with scraps of food and cloth from the big house to share with fellow slaves.

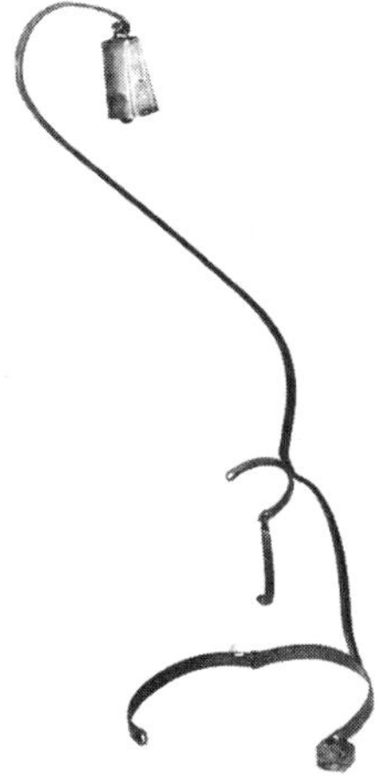

Slave owners used devices like this to harness potential runaways. The bell was several feet above the wearer's head, where he could not reach it, and was designed to alert the owner to the slave's movements. But some slaves managed to muffle the bell with mud.

Ultimately, however, power lay with the owner. Although slaves succeeded in escaping or defied owners in other ways, their fate depended upon the owner's will. An owner could force slaves to marry and even to have children in order to replenish his unpaid labor force, and he could permanently separate families by selling off parents or children. In the 1850s, selling an enslaved child was very profitable for the planter. A newborn child was worth \$100; a five-year-old child brought an owner \$500.

Perhaps the cruelest reminder of their lack of power was a slave mother or father's inability to protect a family member from the

Slave women were pressured by their owners to have many children, who would provide another generation of unpaid laborers.

owner's cruelty. Many a slave wife or mother was forced to stand by silently while her husband or child was whipped. If she intervened, she risked receiving a similar punishment or causing her loved one to receive a more severe punishment. Children also had to watch helplessly as their parents were punished. Caroline Hunter, a former slave from a small farm near Suffolk, Virginia, recalled how as a child she had to watch her mother's beating: "Dey useta strap my mama to a bench or box an' beat her wid a wooden paddle while she was naked." As one former slave woman later recalled, "Lord, Lord . . . ! Them was awful days!"

By the 1840s, however, the idea that slaves were part of the planter's extended family, ruled over by the fatherly figure of the planter, became pervasive. The expression "our family, white and black" appeared constantly in slaveholders' diaries, family correspondence, and recollections of family conversations. Planters told themselves and the world that they loved their slaves. On January 29, 1848, for example, James H. Hammond, a South Carolina planter who was often a harsh master and also an unloving husband and father, nevertheless confided in his diary, "I love my family, and they love me. It is my only earthly tie. It embraces my slaves."

Besides being a way to justify slavery against the growing condemnation of antislavery activists, this idea of one big happy family, ruled over by a firm but benevolent father, was meant to preserve southern society. Southerners regarded the family as the cornerstone of society, the institution that protected all other southern beliefs and traditions, including slavery. Proslavery advocates even declared that men's authority over women and slaves was ordained by God.

As a result, black slave women and white planter women's lives were intertwined, but not as sisters in spirit. They were both subject to the power of the planter but in very different ways. One was his slave, a human workhorse whom he owned. The other was his wife and the mother of his children, the embodiment of purity, innocence, and maternal love. This maternal love, of course, was supposed to extend to her slaves, though it is hard to understand how any woman so imbued with motherly concern could approve of a system that forcibly separated families and brutally treated both children and their parents.

But white women either kept their misgivings hidden in their diaries, simply accepted the harshness of slavery, or actively supported it as loyal Southerners. Slavery benefited them: The free labor extracted from the slave increased the planter's wealth and his ability to provide his wife and children with a comfortable way of life. Slavery was a profitable system of labor that enriched all slave owners, from yeoman farmers to wealthy planters. White planter women had reason, too, to perceive their slaves as "our family, white and black"—such a rosy view of slavery snuffed out any moral unease they may have felt about owning slaves.

In this 1836 engraving entitled "A Planter's Lady," the lady of the house is waited upon by her husband and slave. Ultimately, though, the mistress was responsible for running a smooth household and attending to the needs of her family and slaves.

To be sure, some mistresses felt genuine affection for their slaves—and some slaves, in turn, felt kindly toward owners who treated them well. But the mistress never regarded the slave women who served her as social equals. Her compassion and affection for favorite slaves coexisted with impatience, disdain, and vexation for slaves who did not perform their work to her satisfaction. Many a mistress who spoke fondly of her slaves was not above whipping those who angered her. Mistresses could be as brutal as their husbands when they punished slaves.

Especially did they lash out at female slaves whom their husbands exploited sexually. Many planters followed a sexual double standard: While extolling the sexual purity of white women, they forced themselves on black women. This was perhaps the cruelest aspect of slavery for both black slave women and white planter women. Slave girls as young as 13 or 14 were forced to fend off the unwelcome sexual advances of their masters.

Many female slaves had no choice but to submit to masters or overseers—or be brutally beaten or sold. One woman recalled how the overseer tied her mother by the arms to the barn rafters and beat her until "the blood run down her back to her heels"—simply because she would not submit to his sexual advances. Another woman remembered how her sister described being raped by several white men: "They'd make her go out and lay on a table and two or three

The planter seated at right is selling his own mulatto son (standing left). Liaisons between white planters and their slave women were frequent, resulting in mulatto children. The planter had fathered not only his illegitimate son but his property.

white men would have sex with her before they'd let her up. She was just a small girl. She died when she was still in her young days."

For a planter's wife, perhaps the most humiliating—and certainly the most visible—outcome of a sexual liaison between her husband and a female slave was the mulatto offspring. Few planter women wanted to acknowledge these children as evidence of their husbands' unfaithfulness to them. As Mary Boykin Chesnut, a slaveholder's wife who was a keen observer of southern planter life, tartly remarked, "Any lady is ready to tell you who is the father of all the mulatto children in everybody's household but her own. Those, she seems to think, drop from the clouds." But that did not prevent mistresses from mistreating the children of those illicit relations. They sometimes sold these children away from their mothers or treated them viciously.

Mistresses exerted firm control over their household slaves. One young slave reported being whipped by her mistress, who was furious that the child had dared to play with one of her children's toys.

Despite popular images of the mistress as a genteel lady of leisure who spent her days doing delicate needlework and sipping mint juleps on the veranda, the realities of her life were very different. Just as the family was the cornerstone of society, the planter household was the economic and moral foundation of southern life—and the mistress stood at the center of this foundation. She supervised the entire range of domestic operations on the farm or plantation, from cooking and sewing to ministering to the physical needs and religious salvation of her family and slaves. Some women, especially very wealthy planters' wives who had a retinue of household slaves, did indeed enjoy a more leisurely, mannered life of visiting, strolling around their plantations, doing needlework, and entertaining. But to have time for these pleasant pursuits, they had to be superb administrators who nimbly knew how to delegate tasks to household slaves.

Most planter women, however, worked almost as hard as their slaves—although they had far more control over the conditions and amount of their work. They rose early and did not finish the day's work until well after sunset. They had to oversee morning meals, order supplies for the larder, supervise the slaughter of animals and smoking of meat, organize the house cleaning, assess the clothing needs of family and slaves—sometimes sewing the clothing themselves—tend to their gardens, and nurse sick family members and slaves.

"A home on the Mississippi" about 1850, as depicted in a romantic engraving by Currier & Ives. For slaves, of course, life was not so idyllic.

The December 29, 1860, diary entry of Meta Morris Grimball, the wife of a South Carolina planter, suggests the many tasks and demands of a typical day: "This morning I got up late having been disturbed in the night, hurried down to have something arranged for breakfast, Ham & eggs, . . . wrote a letter to Charles . . . had prayers, got the boys off to town. Had work cut out, gave orders about dinner, had the horse feed fixed in hot water, had the box filled with cork; went to see about the carpenters working at the negro houses . . . & now I have to cut out the flannel jackets." On her birthday in 1859, Sarah R. Espy, an Alabama mistress, recorded in her diary that she helped her slaves slaughter 15 large hogs. The next day, she put up 22 gallons of lard in addition to other tasks.

Wealthier women also pursued charity activities. They donated cast-off clothing to poor white women, especially widows, visited sick women, and distributed Bibles. Doing good works was a way to confirm their upper-class status. But other than extending charity to poor white women, wealthy planter women deliberately kept their distance from them.

Such a full life devoted to family and plantation cares and to good works hardly offered much leisure time. For most planter women, there were simply not enough hours in the day to keep the plantation running smoothly. But somewhere between slaughtering the hogs and supervising the spinning, planter women found time to express themselves passionately on the issues of the day. A British traveler observed after a dinner party in Columbia, South Carolina, "I had as tough an argument with some of the ladies over slavery as ever Basil [her husband] had on any subject with the gentlemen." Another visitor found southern women "more irritable and violent than their men on political questions." Many women were as ardently devoted to the southern way of life as their men. As the South lurched closer to Civil War, they were among those who rallied loudest for secession.

But some women privately detested slavery—in part out of genuine concern for the slaves' plight but also because they felt enslaved along with their human property. "I cannot, nor will not, spend all these precious days of my life following after and watching Negroes," Laura Beecher Comer of North Carolina proclaimed in her diary during the war. "It is a terrible life!" In 1859, Ella Gertrude Clanton Thomas, a planter's wife from Georgia, wrote in her diary, "Southern women are all, I believe, abolitionists."

However strong these antislavery sentiments were, or however dissatisfied they felt with their lives, southern women kept their feelings to themselves or confided them to trusted friends and relatives. Only a few went North to join the antislavery movement, as Sarah and Angelina Grimké of South Carolina did, or bought slaves to send them to freedom in Liberia, as Mary Berkeley Minor Blackford of Virginia did. Most southern women who felt morally uneasy about slavery, or were simply fed up with the demands and limitations of their lives, silently bore their discontent.

Many white Southern women read with a passion for knowledge of the world beyond their busy households. After a long, laborious day of plantation chores, they tackled Shakespeare, Greek and Roman history, and other weighty subjects.

Some women channeled this discontent into a rigorous program of self-education because they had so few opportunities to acquire a formal education. Public schools did not spring up in the antebellum, or pre-Civil War, South as they did in the North. Instead, women embarked upon ambitious reading and writing programs. A young mother from Georgia reported in her journal in 1857 that she had been reading the essays of Thomas Macaulay, a British historian and author. The essays inspired her to read more because she felt so ignorant. "I must and will devote more time to study," she declared.

Other women reported in their diaries that they were studying Latin and working their way through the Bible, the collected works of Shakespeare, Greek and Roman history, and the latest scientific theories, such as Darwin's view of natural selection. Their diaries

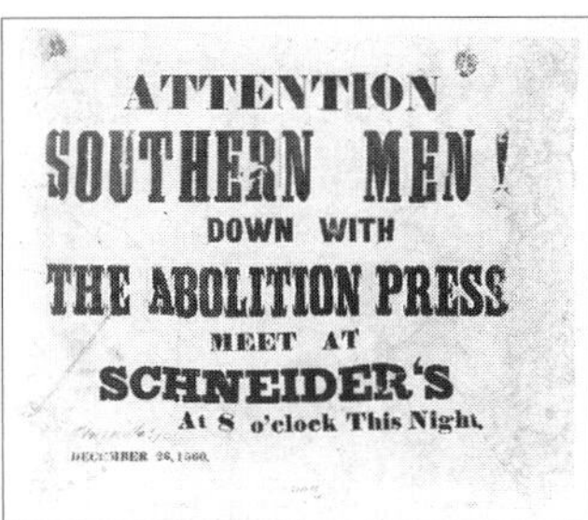

This handbill announced a meeting in Augusta, Georgia, to protest the influx of abolitionist literature. In their haste to rally their fellow citizens, the organizers misprinted the date.

are filled with lengthy and astute reactions to their reading. Women also read novels. These stories of romance and adventure, of faraway places and distant times fed their imaginations and craving for the world outside of their busy households.

Beyond the big house and the slave quarters lived another group of people whose lives were almost as precarious as those of the slaves: free African Americans. Their numbers were small compared to their enslaved sisters and brothers. By 1860, there were 250,000 free blacks in the South compared to nearly 4 million African-American slaves. Unlike northern blacks, free blacks in the South risked losing their freedom if they visibly supported antislavery efforts. Many lamented the plight of slaves, and some endangered their lives by working for the Underground Railroad. But most free blacks tried to represent themselves as honest, hard-working people who had no intention of helping to abolish slavery.

Racism among all white Southerners, from the wealthiest planters to the lowliest farmers, and their suspicions that free blacks would naturally oppose slavery, made the lives of free blacks very uncertain. Some whites even believed that they should be enslaved. In 1851, George Fitzhugh, a leading southern thinker who ardently supported slavery, declared, "Humanity, self-interest, [and] consistency all require that we should enslave the free negro."

Many years earlier, in 1820, Thomas Jefferson spoke of his fears that the nation could not long tolerate the growing conflict between opponents and supporters of slavery. Like a "fire bell in the night," Jefferson wrote, the unresolved question of slavery had aroused him and "filled me with terror. I considered it at once as the knell of the Union." Slavery, he feared, would embroil the entire country in a fiery conflict. In the two decades preceding the Civil War, slaveholders clung ever more insistently on what they proclaimed as their constitutional right to own other human beings. In turn, opponents of slavery argued more fiercely for its demise.

In 1850, a new compromise passed by the U.S. Congress temporarily patched up these growing differences. Under the Compromise of 1850, as it came to be called, Congress admitted the new state of California into the Union as a free state—a state in which slavery was prohibited. In addition, legislatures in the territories of New Mexico and Utah were to decide whether to allow slavery there.

After the new fugitive slave law was passed, antislavery proponents (such as William Lloyd Garrison, depicted at left) watched in horror as blacks, who had been living and working in free states for many years, were captured and returned to slavery.

Congress also abolished the slave trade, but not slavery itself, in Washington, D.C., and passed a more stringent fugitive slave law.

Unlike previous fugitive slave laws, this new law enabled slave owners to track down runaway slaves in free states and return them to slavery more easily. Fugitive slaves now had a harder time proving their claim to freedom, and slave owners had more legal power on their side. The law also imposed stiff penalties on anyone who harbored a fugitive or prevented officials from capturing a runaway. Antislavery proponents watched in horror as blacks, who had been living and working in free states for many years, were captured and returned to slavery. This law aroused fierce opposition to slavery throughout the North.

Women of both races were swept up in the growing national debate over slavery. From as early as the 1820s, women in the North had joined antislavery organizations and had begun to work for the slaves' freedom. In the antislavery cause, they became aware of the many ways in which they, too, were not free. By the late 1840s, many women had found a cause as dear to their hearts as the slaves' liberation—their own social, political, and economic equality. As the nation inched closer to Civil War over slavery, American women began to wage their own battle for the rights and privileges of being American citizens.

CHAPTER 2

"EVERY FIBRE OF MY BEING REBELLED": A MOVEMENT FOR WOMEN'S RIGHTS BEGINS

Early in the morning of July 19, 1848, the clip-clop of horses' hooves and the rumble of carriage wheels over dirt paths could be heard throughout Seneca Falls, a quiet country village nestled in the Finger Lakes region of upstate New York. Usually a placid country village, Seneca Falls churned with activity on this fine summer morning. From all around the region, people—especially women—converged upon the small town.

Why did all of these women head toward this normally sleepy outpost? Some had come out of curiosity, but others had a more serious purpose in mind—to demand equality for themselves and for other American women. The first convention dedicated to achieving women's rights was about to begin.

It had been eight years since Elizabeth Cady Stanton and Lucretia Mott, two of the convention's organizers, had first proposed such a meeting. In 1840, Stanton had met Mott at the first World Anti-slavery Convention in London, England. At that convention, women delegates—dedicated and hard-working volunteers seeking to abolish the cruel institution of slavery—were seated separately from the men and were not permitted to address the convention. Both Stanton and Mott, who were American delegates, were outraged. Walking arm in arm through London, as Stanton later recalled, they "resolved to hold a convention as soon as we returned home, and form a society to advocate the rights of women."

Some mid-19th-century American women were fearless crusaders for a variety of causes, notably women's rights and temperance. Relishing new public roles, they ultimately rode into battle during the Civil War.

Lucretia Mott, a highly respected Quaker reformer and abolitionist, was a woman of deep principle who fervently believed in women's social and political equality. Her younger colleague Elizabeth Cady Stanton called her "an entire new revelation of womanhood."

Yet, back home in the United States, Stanton often felt overwhelmed with the cares of housekeeping and raising three young children. Finally, several years later, she visited Lucretia Mott, who was staying with friends in a town near Seneca Falls. Over tea, as she later recalled in her autobiography, she poured out her frustration "with such vehemence and indignation that I stirred myself, as well as the rest of the party, to do and dare anything." What the five women, including Stanton, dared to do was organize a convention.

Stanton, Mott, and the other three women sitting around that tea table—Martha Wright, Jane Hunt, and Mary Ann McClintock—issued a call in the *Seneca County Courier* for a two-day convention devoted to the question of "the social, civil, and religious condition and rights of woman." Initially, the five organizers of the Seneca Falls convention felt overwhelmed by the task of trying to put into words the injustices that women had suffered. As they set about writing the declaration, Stanton later said, they felt "as helpless and hopeless as if they had been suddenly asked to construct a steam engine."

They consulted several "masculine productions" before turning to the Declaration of Independence for inspiration. They adapted the Preamble of the Declaration of Independence and listed their grievances just as the authors of that earlier declaration had done. In this way, they hoped to provide their cause with the same moral and political justifications that had inspired the American Revolution. Like the Founding Fathers, they sought to overthrow an unjust power—in this case, the social and political rule of men—that had deprived them of their equal rights and their pursuit of a life of liberty and happiness.

A married woman's right to keep her property, including her earnings if she worked, was one of many demands that the organizers made in their manifesto, "The Declaration of Sentiments and Resolutions." They also demanded the end of a legal tradition that prevented married women from signing contracts, that gave fathers instead of mothers guardianship over their children in divorce proceedings, that denied women a voice in making laws, and that compelled wives to obey their husbands in all matters. They also called for greater educational and employment opportunities for women.

They also insisted that men no longer decide what social roles were appropriate for women—a right that "belongs to her conscience and to her God," according to the declaration—and that women be granted the right to vote. This last demand was the most radical because it directly challenged women's subservience to men, and put women on an equal plane with men as citizens of the republic. Never before had American women publicly demanded such a right. Even Lucretia Mott, a firm believer in women's equality, gasped when she first read this demand in the declaration. She exclaimed to Stanton, who had drafted most of the declaration, "Oh, Lizzie, thou will make us ridiculous! We must go slowly." But Stanton would not budge, and the demand for women's suffrage stayed in.

Fearing that the demands of the summer haying season would draw potential participants away, the five organizers were astounded when, on July 19, about 300 people, including 40 men, showed up for the convention. Among those attending was Charlotte Woodward, a young glovemaker who wanted to change the laws that gave husbands the right to pocket their wives' earnings and any property they owned. "Most women," she wrote later, "accepted this condition of society as normal and God-ordained and therefore changeless. But . . . every fibre of my being rebelled, although silently, all the hours that I sat and sewed gloves for a miserable pittance which, after it was earned, could never be mine." Woodward wanted to work, she explained, "but I wanted to choose my task and I wanted to collect my wages."

Following a vigorous discussion of the issues, on the second day the participants voted on the declaration and the resolutions. All of the resolutions passed unanimously—except for the one demanding women's suffrage, the right to vote. Like Lucretia Mott, the participants feared that such a radical demand would arouse public opposition to their cause. But Stanton held firm, insisting that the ability to vote would enable women to achieve their other demands more quickly.

Frederick Douglass, a former slave and an ardent supporter of women's rights, agreed with her. Douglass, who had escaped from slavery and had become one of the most compelling speakers for the antislavery movement, was editor of the *North Star,* one of the first successful newspapers published by an African American. He supported women's rights as part of a quest to achieve freedom and

Only after hearing a compelling speech by Frederick Douglass did the delegates to the Seneca Falls convention vote in favor of the resolution for woman suffrage.

REPORT

OF THE

WOMAN'S RIGHTS

CONVENTION,

Held at SENECA FALLS, N. Y., July 19th and 20th, 1848.

ROCHESTER:
PRINTED BY JOHN DICK,
AT THE NORTH STAR OFFICE.

1848.

Elizabeth Cady Stanton proclaimed the Seneca Falls convention a "grand success," and the organizers scheduled another convention for two weeks later in Rochester, New York, where this report was printed.

equality for all people, and he regarded women's suffrage as an essential tool for winning women's own freedom and equality. Now, as a participant at the Seneca Falls convention, he helped Stanton defend the suffrage demand. After further debate, the resolution passed by a small margin. At the end of the final session, 100 women and men—including Charlotte Woodward, the young glovemaker—signed the Declaration of Sentiments and Resolutions.

Newspapers across the country carried reports of the Seneca Falls convention. Much of the coverage was critical, even nasty. One editorial called the convention "the most shocking and unnatural incident ever recorded in the history of womanity." Editors accused female participants of "unwomanly behavior" and of neglecting "their more appropriate duties." They feared that equal rights would "demoralize and degrade" women and "prove a monstrous injury to all mankind."

The newspapers' disparaging coverage frightened some people away. A few signers of the Declaration of Sentiments and Resolutions withdrew their support because of all the publicity, and others even spurned the organizers of the Seneca Falls convention. Still other women who did indeed support the cause of women's rights could not resist their husbands' opposition. But some women were not so easily cowed, and the convention galvanized them to work for women's rights.

Seneca Falls was the opening salvo in the organized women's rights movement in the United States. At Seneca Falls, women had finally set forth the problem of sexual inequality in all of its forms—political, social, economic, and personal—and organized a movement to combat this inequality. The Declaration of Sentiments became a road map for the path they hoped to travel toward equality and self-determination. It would set the tone and goals of the American women's rights movement for decades to come. More important, the convention brought women together as a group to solve their problems. After Seneca Falls, women would convene other conventions and eventually establish local and national organizations to press their claims. From now on, American women would crusade for their rights behind the banner of an organized movement.

Perhaps it was not coincidental that the Seneca Falls convention was held in 1848—a year in which revolutions and insurrections

The campaign against alcohol was one of the earliest and largest women's reform movements. Temperance advocates viewed alcohol abuse as a threat not only to the drinking men themselves but to their wives and families.

swept Europe. In France, the people overthrew their king and established a republic headed by a president. Eighteen forty-eight was also a year of significant changes in the United States. The spirit of progress and reform abounded. The antislavery movement, the temperance movement to rid the country of the scourge of alcohol, and various experiments in communal living—all of these movements attempted to create a more enlightened and democratic society.

Although the Seneca Falls convention launched an organized women's rights movement in America, the ideas expressed at Seneca Falls—and the anger at women's inferior political and social status so eloquently voiced in the Declaration of Sentiments and Resolu-

Young women at work in a valentine factory about 1850. Many women took their domestic skills from home to factory.

tions—had been simmering for a long time. These ideas and sentiments had found earlier expression in the writings of courageous women who had rejected the social and legal restrictions imposed upon their sex, and in the blossoming awareness of women who had joined the antislavery movement and charitable societies.

As the growing nation relied more on factories in the Northeast, mainly in Rhode Island, Massachusetts, New York, and Pennsylvania, to produce its goods, many women had more time for such activities. They no longer wove the cloth for their family's apparel or made candles or soap or any of the other goods their families used. Some women, especially young, single women, worked in the factories that made these goods, while other women continued to work at home, sewing for their own families as well as for manufacturers who paid them by the piece.

While enjoying the fruits of the new industrial order, such as ready-made goods, married women also played a new role—as nurturing, maternal wives and mothers. The harsh realm of business and manufacture made men and women see the home as a sanctuary, a place in which the values of love, harmony, and virtue reigned—a gentle, loving refuge from the harsh world outside. Women were expected to rule over this domain of love and peace.

This role invested women with special power and influence. "To render home happy is woman's peculiar province, home is her world," gushed the *Ladies' Magazine* in 1830. But home was expected to be her only province—the world out there was too rough and tumble for her tender mercies. Popular books and magazines and religious and intellectual leaders increasingly assigned two separate roles, or spheres, to men and women: the active world of business and politics for men, and the more peaceful and private sphere of the home and family for women. Some women bristled at these rigid restrictions on their lives. They wanted to be part of the world beyond their front doors, and they risked the disapproval of family and friends to seek an education, acquire a skill or pursue a profession, and forgo marriage.

Other women, both married and single, took another path toward participating in that world: They formed or joined moral reform and charitable organizations, because they wanted to make their communities as virtuous and caring as their own homes. In these organizations, mostly centered in the small towns and cities of the Northeast, they tried to instill higher moral standards among the "fallen," such as prostitutes, and dispensed charity to the needy. During the antebellum era, roughly from 1830 to the Civil War, these and other kinds of voluntary organizations flourished.

In their groups, women developed important organizational and leadership skills. They learned how to draft their own constitutions and bylaws, elected officers, organized meetings and assigned duties, managed funds, and wrote and published progress reports. They also learned how to distribute petitions and testify before courts

In the "Home of the Temperate," as this engraving was originally captioned, a man stayed home in the evening to read to his children.

The Female Association of Philadelphia for the Relief of the Sick and Infirm Poor with Clothing was founded in 1852. This ledger shows the name of each recipient, the number of items of clothing received, and the name of the distributor.

Mary Gross	3	
Isabella Lovealt	8	Helen G Longstreth
Betsy Dubois Col	1	
Louisa Orum Col	2	
Mary Clincher Col	6	S. R Gillingham
Hannah Sullivan	4	
Catherine Buttler	4	
Jane Richers	8	
Ann Williams	8	
Ann Johnson	6	Hannah Miller
Suffa family	7	Elizabeth White
Sarah Grey	4	E A Bunting
Rachel Gray	2	
Rebecca Turner	2	
—— Williams	2	Sarah Blorbit
Peacock family	8	E A Bunting
Catherine Johnson & child	7	
Mary Johns Col	4	
Sarah Emerson Col	2	S R Gillingham

and state legislative committees. These and other newly acquired organizational skills instilled pride and self-confidence. In 1837, a volunteer for one organization exulted, "I rejoice my friends that I am woman; and I never gloried more in my sex than I do now."

Perhaps more importantly, women volunteers learned about the many difficulties that other women faced. They distributed firewood to widows, dispensed medicine to the sick, raised funds for orphanages, and tried to convert nonbelievers to Christianity. They also established training schools, nurseries, employment facilities, hospitals, and shelters for women and children. From these many volunteer tasks and others, they learned firsthand about the problems of women's lives—from meager earnings that hardly supported female wage earners to husbands and employers who were cruel or irresponsible. In this way, they began to challenge men's authority and to suggest ways that women could improve their lives.

African-American women as well as white women formed associations in the antebellum years. Most African-American clubs were formed in northern states, where slavery had died out or been abolished. But a few clubs for freed blacks existed in the slaveholding South as well. Most African-American clubs were educational in purpose. By 1849, more than half of Philadelphia's African-American population, men as well as women, belonged to one of 106 black literary organizations in the city.

Other black clubs helped the African-American community by building schools and libraries for their people. The Ohio Ladies Education Society, a club formed by black women in 1837, had a sterling record of accomplishment. By the 1840s, it had opened more schools for African Americans than any other black, or white, organization in the nation. African-American women and men defied poverty and racism to organize clubs that served their communities. Their impressive club activities were even more remarkable because of the obstacles they overcame.

African-American women discovered their strength and power as women through helping themselves and their communities. In the 1830s, their chief advocate was Maria Stewart, a black woman. She was also the first American-born woman to lecture in public—an

Free black citizens were devoted to educating both black children and adults. Even in the North, however, their schools were subject to attack.

activity simply not pursued by any other woman of her day. In her lectures, Stewart urged black women to help strengthen the African-American community. "Daughters of Africa, awake!" Stewart exhorted her audience in Boston's Franklin Hall on September 21, 1832. "Arise! Distinguish yourselves. O do not say, you cannot make anything of your children; but say, with the help and assistance of God, we will try."

By 1833, Stewart's public-speaking activities had aroused such intense opposition among Boston's black leaders that she decided to leave the city. To them, more troubling than her message was the fact that she was a woman who had dared to speak in public. Before she left, she defended her right as a woman to speak out: "What if I am a woman; is not the God of ancient times the God of these modern days? Did he not raise up Deborah to be a mother and a judge in Israel? Did not Queen Esther save the lives of the Jews? And Mary Magdalene first declare the resurrection of Christ from the dead?" Stewart spoke from the depths of her soul. She was a towering example of courage and drive to other African-American women who wanted to improve their own lives and help their people.

From the abolitionist movement, which sought to abolish slavery in the South, women acquired a philosophy and a vocabulary of equality. Like moral reform and charity work, abolition reflected the temper of the times—a fervent desire to improve society, to end injustice and inequality. In 1832, in Salem, Massachusetts, and Rochester, New York, African-American women organized the first female antislavery societies in America. Like black women's mutual aid and literary groups, these antislavery societies believed that African Americans must improve their lives themselves. The constitution of the Woman's Association of Philadelphia, for example, claimed "Self-Elevation to be the only true issue upon which to base our efforts as an oppressed portion of the American people." The women linked the success of their cause to their "Self-Exertion" as fighters for the abolition of slavery and crusaders against racial prejudice.

One year later, in 1833, Lucretia Mott and other white women organized a Female Antislavery Society in Philadelphia after they were prohibited from voting in the newly organized American Antislavery Society. Throughout New England and the Midwest, women organized other all-female antislavery societies. These societies chan-

CIRCULAR.

THE FIRST REPORT OF THE ROCHESTER LADIES' ANTI-SLAVERY SEWING SOCIETY.

TREASURER'S REPORT.

Amount of Receipts at the Anti-Slavery Fair, March 18th and 19th, 1852.

For Foreign goods sold	$114,02
" Domestic "	38,76
" Books	19,00
" Refreshments	103,47
" Entrance at door	66,26
" Donations from Philadelphia	10,00
" " McGrawville	10,00
" " Peterboro	5,00
" " Canandaigua	11,00
" " Rochester	31,12
	$408,57

Charges.		
Paid Mr. Reynolds for Hall	$50,00	
Sundry Bills	49,36	
		99,36
		$309,21
Donation to Mr. Douglass		233,00
Balance in Treasury		76,21

MARIA G. PORTER, *Treasurer.*

This report stated, "The sum realized, though quite small, when, viewed in connection with our large wishes, and the pressing wants of the anti-slavery cause, is, nevertheless, highly encouraging." It acknowledged the contributions of "friends on both sides of the Atlantic."

neled their discontent with the limited domestic scope of their lives, and enabled them to feel they were contributing to their society. By 1837, 77 out of 1,000 antislavery societies were exclusively female. A few societies were racially integrated, but most were composed of either black or white women.

All of these organizations confronted intense opposition—in part because the opposition of slavery itself was an unpopular cause, especially William Lloyd Garrison's more militant branch of abolitionism. Garrison demanded immediate emancipation of all slaves instead of a gradual emancipation by region or state. But an abolitionist organization composed only of women was too much for many people to bear. At their meetings, these groups often faced hostile mobs. Yet, undaunted, the women went about their work. They circulated petitions asking northern state legislatures to grant citizenship to black inhabitants, did fund-raising to pay for legal counsel or the freedom of runaway slaves, worked with the Underground Railroad, and spoke in public.

Antislavery women drew heavily on the precepts of William Lloyd Garrison. He regarded blacks and whites as equal human beings who were entitled to the same rights and privileges. Antislavery women applied this principle to men and women. They challenged a socialorder based on sexual inequality, claiming that women, as human beings, were the equal of men and therefore deserved equal rights. They denied that women were destined to play a submissive role.

Pennsylvania Hall was built after none of the Philadelphia churches or Quaker meetings would allow their buildings to be used for abolitionist meetings. Opened on May 14, 1838, it was burned to the ground three days later.

Antislavery women were also inspired by the Quakers, who were staunch abolitionists. In addition, Quakers believed that women and men, alike, possessed an "inner light," a conscience that enabled them to grasp the deepest moral truths and live as equally moral and responsible human beings. In contrast, most Christian denominations did not believe that men and women should play an equal social or religious role; instead, they believed that women's social and religious subservience was divinely ordained.

Finally, antislavery women drew on precepts of natural, undeniable rights. These precepts, first espoused by French philosophers in the 18th century, are embodied in the Declaration of Independence and declare that all persons are equally entitled to life, liberty, and the pursuit of happiness. Just as a black slave was a person with the inalienable rights of self-determination and citizenship, antislavery women argued, so was a woman a person with these same rights.

Sarah and Angelina Grimké, for example, found their way to the cause of women's rights through their antislavery work. The Grimké sisters, who were daughters of a South Carolina slave owner, were deeply troubled by the brutality of slavery. They left the South for Philadelphia, where they became Quakers, joined the Philadelphia Female Antislavery Society, and began to give talks in private homes about the immorality of slavery. They were such compelling speakers that invitations to lecture soon flowed in from all over the Northeast. Embarking upon a lecture tour, the sisters traveled throughout New York and Massachusetts to address groups of women and, eventually, men.

But they encountered opposition to their public speaking, and they rose up in protest. Like Maria Stewart, they defended the right of a woman to act, in their words, as "a moral, intelligent and responsible being." Sarah Grimké even wrote a series of letters on "The Province of Woman" for the *New England Spectator*. In 1838, she published the letters in book form as *Letters on the Equality of the Sexes*. "Men and women were CREATED EQUAL," she declared. "They are both moral and accountable beings, and whatever is *right* for man to do, is *right* for woman."

Margaret Fuller was another shining advocate of women's rights during this time. Like others, she bemoaned the lack of attention given to women's intellectual development. A precocious child who could read Latin at the age of six, the young Margaret Fuller matured into a vibrant woman for whom the life of the mind was more important than anything else. "I must die," she once said, "if I do not burst forth in genius or heroism."

One way she chose to burst forth was by helping women improve their intellectual skills. To this end, starting in 1839, she offered a series of "Conversations" at a bookstore in Boston. In these two-hour sessions, open only to women, Fuller briefly introduced the topic of the day and then led a discussion. Every member had to participate—not merely as idle chatterers but as thoughtful participants prepared to defend their points of view. For the next five years, Fuller conducted her Conversations to full classes of women.

The ideas of the visionary Margaret Fuller contributed greatly to the women's rights movement. She wrote: "I would have woman lay aside all thought...of being taught and led by men. I would have her free from compromise, from complaisance, from helplessness."

In 1845, she codified her thoughts on women's potential in her book *Woman in the Nineteenth Century*. In it, she offered a remarkably advanced vision of women's lives. She rejected the idea of a designated and limited sphere of activity and urged women to seek an education and work at whatever they desired: "Let them be sea-captains, if they will." She exhorted women to educate themselves for their own benefit, not merely to be better wives and mothers.

One young woman who heeded Fuller's words to seek an education was Lucy Stone. Born on a farm in western Massachusetts in

In her public speeches, Lucy Stone addressed the problems of women as well as blacks. "I was a woman before I was an abolitionist," she said. "I must speak for the women."

1818, Stone was the third girl in a family of seven surviving children. When her overworked mother learned that her new baby was a girl, she moaned, "Oh, dear! I am sorry it is a girl. A woman's life is so hard." Although the Stone daughters performed their fair share of work on the family's farm, their father, who was rigid and authoritarian, did not believe they deserved the same educational opportunities as their brothers; thus he sent his sons to college but not his daughters. Lucy pleaded with him to lend her the money to continue her schooling. He grudgingly agreed—only after she promised to sign a note for the loan.

For the next several years, young Lucy Stone attended classes and taught school to repay her father. She attended Mount Holyoke Seminary in western Massachusetts and then Oberlin College in Ohio. Oberlin, which opened in 1833, was the first college to accept both women and African Americans. Working part time and living meagerly, Stone struggled to stay in college.

Gradually, she became more aware of the inequalities that women suffered, and at Oberlin she quickly gained a reputation as a troublemaker. With Antoinette Brown, a dear friend and fellow student, she fought to gain more rights for women at Oberlin, such as being allowed to give public addresses and participate in debates.

At graduation, Lucy Stone decided to become a professional public speaker. When her family objected to this "unladylike" vocation, she wrote, "I expect to plead not for the slave only, but for suffering humanity everywhere. Especially do I mean to labor for the elevation of my sex." In the spring of 1848, Stone embarked on a career as a speaker for the Massachusetts Antislavery Society. She mesmerized audiences with her soft musical voice; one listener remarked that it sounded "like a silver bell."

Like other abolitionists, she was harassed wherever she spoke. Opponents tore down the posters advertising her talks, threw pepper into the auditoriums where she lectured, and even doused her with cold water one winter day. But, like the Grimké sisters, she insisted on her right to speak out—in support of abolition and women's rights. When the Massachusetts Antislavery Society protested that she had been hired to speak only on abolition, she retorted, "I was a woman before I was an abolitionist. I must speak for the women."

The path to Seneca Falls, therefore, was paved by many courageous women who, like Stone, chose to speak for their sex—who had refused in thought or deed to accept the social, legal, and political inequalities that hindered women's lives. Two weeks after the convention, in early August 1848, another group of women organized a convention in Rochester, New York. At this meeting, a woman, the Quaker Abigail Bush, chaired the proceedings. Even Elizabeth Cady Stanton was doubtful about this unusual practice and called it a "hazardous experiment." But Bush's superb leadership skills quickly won her over. From then on, women chaired their own conventions. At the Rochester convention, participants debated a resolution on woman suffrage, and this time it passed with a wider margin.

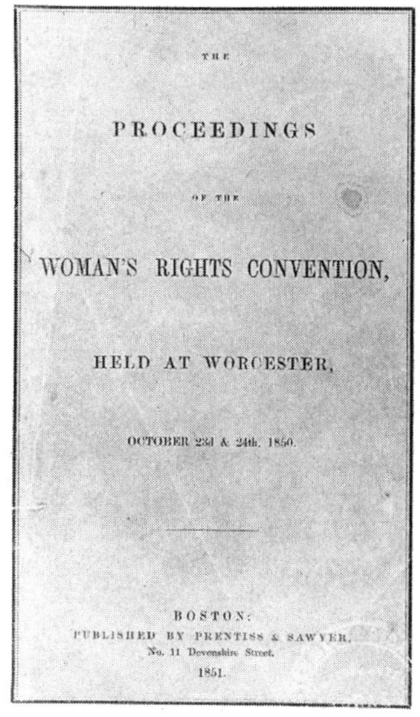

THE

PROCEEDINGS

OF THE

WOMAN'S RIGHTS CONVENTION,

HELD AT WORCESTER,

OCTOBER 23d & 24th, 1850.

BOSTON:
PUBLISHED BY PRENTISS & SAWYER,
No. 11 Devonshire Street.
1851.

At the Worcester convention, delegates decided to submit suffrage petitions to eight state legislatures. Women's right to vote had now become the central goal of the women's rights movement.

After this convention, activists did not organize another convention for a year and a half. In April 1850, women gathered in Salem, Ohio; six months later, in October 1850, the first National Woman's Rights Convention was held in Worcester, Massachusetts.

As the new decade unfolded, the ripple effect of women's demands for equality spread, and new leaders and fresh visions of women's lives emerged. American women would not be stopped in their crusade to achieve their political rights and their full potential as human beings. They had crossed a barrier, and they would not be held back from entering that active arena of life.

A Paper Devoted to the Elevation of Woman.

"OUT OF THE GREAT HEART OF NATURE SEEK WE TRUTH."

VOL II. PROVIDENCE, R. I., DECEMBER, 1854. NO. 12.

THE UNA,

PUBLISHED MONTHLY, AT PROVIDENCE, R. I.

Subscription Price, One Dollar per annum in advance.

☞Persons desiring the paper, can have six copies sent to one address for five dollars.

☞All communications designed for the paper or on business, to be addressed to

Mrs. Paulina Wright Davis, Editor and Proprietor.

SAYLES, MILLER & SIMONS, PRINTERS.

For the Una.

LESSONS OF LIFE.

Chapter VII.

These eyes though clear,
To outward view, of blemish or of spot,
Bereft of light, their seeing, have forgot;
Nor to their idle orbs doth sight appear
Of sun, or moon, or star throughout the year,
Or man or woman. Yet I argue not
Against heaven's hand or will, nor bate a jot
Of heart or hope; but still bear up, and speed
Right onward.

We rode home by the glowing light of the July sunset; and alas, I saw that to the eye of my beloved friend, it beamed in vain. Hamilton, an enthusiastic lover of nature, poured forth his delight in poetry and speech; her hand pressed mine convulsively as she listened.

As we went to her room to prepare for tea I could bear this reserve no longer. I threw my arms around her neck, exclaiming, "O, Marian, is it indeed so! Why did you hide it from me. Could I not help you to bear it?"

"You have helped me, Margaret," she said. "Yes, it is so, I am blind. I cannot see your dear face, which I know is beaming kindly on me, and, to-night the radiance of the setting sun I could not see. But the bitterness is past, I can bear it."

I could only lay my head, weeping, on her shoulder, it seemed at first too heavy for her to bear; but she rebuked me with gentle love. "I must tell Hamilton to night, she said, and —Henry—Let me reserve my strength for that. Will you not help me? Do not make our supper sad, it is Hamilton's day."

Henry had left to return later in the evening and Marian sat down at the table cheerful and calm. I in vain attempted to imitate her composure, and Hamilton laughed at me, that my first visit to the imposing university had quite overcome me. We sat a little while in the twilight. When the lights were brought in Hamilton rose to move them. "These will hurt your eyes Marian" he said. "No Hamilton, they will not hurt me, let them stay, I cannot see them."

The lamp he held would have fallen had I not taken it.

"Dearest Marian, he said, what can you mean?" "I mean that I am blind; even the bright setting sun I could not see."

"Blind!" He came to her and looked so earnestly in her face. She returned not his look and such an expression of agony came there as I had never seen before.

"Marian," he said, "can you not see me?"

"No Hamilton, only in my heart. I can feel your presence round me, but your face is hid forever." He turned and laid his head upon the table, and we could hear the sobs which rent his bosom. Marian's fortitude failed before it. "Lead me to him," she said, "I did so." She leaned upon his shoulder and said, "Dear Hamilton, you have been my strength in every trial, will you fail me now?"

"God forgive me," he said, "but oh, Marian, I loved you so much, I have been so proud of you, I have looked forward to the day that you should show forth all the greatness and power of your intellect to the world. I am not ambitious for myself; I have been for you—and this withering blight—Oh, Marian, would I could take this cup from you!"

"Do not say so, Hamilton; but why should you grieve so deeply? It is not a little thing, but to the soul it is nothing. If I have a true message to speak, shall it not come with deeper force from the soul baptised into sorrow? Can I not more freely speak and act? I feel that I have new power. The fatal consequence of my own impatience, this teacher comes to read me her sublime lesson, and all that in other hours I have sown in my soul will now bear fruit in my life."

"Let me help you," said he, "let me be your sight, your scribe, your companion, your friend. Oh Marion, how can I relieve you of this burthen."

"Be still as ever my best, my dearest brother," she said. She held a hand of each of us. "Will you call me poor," she said, "with two such friends, who have given me inward sight. I would not lose you, to regain this whole fair universe of outward beauty."

"Come let us sit beside the window," she said, "I can still enjoy the Honeysuckle's breath, and we will talk more sweetly there." Margaret will you repeat for me Milton's great sonnet.

"When I consider how my light is spent
Ere half my days in this dark world and wide" and—

I did so and as I closed she said—"What noble truth! Were it not worth a life of darkness to see God thus—Hamilton, shall I ever attain to this?"

Tears fell upon his cheek as he said, "You are not far from the kingdom of God."

Henry joined us and at Marian's request he passed the evening mostly in singing. She was quiet and cheerful and looked forward with a sweet and frank hope. As we parted she said to me. "You will tell Henry all—I could once— but a poor blind girl—no I will put away the cup, I would not be a burden to him."

I did tell him, but he was not surprised. "I have watched her too closely to be deceived. I have seen her struggles, her victory, and my heart has bled for her. Oh Margaret, can I do aught for her? I have given her my whole heart, will it bless her? Now when she needs it so much shall I take from her her support and ask her to share my poverty. Can my love make her happy?"

"What has Earth so great and rich?" I said, "God bless you both!"

I felt that the morrow would decide my fate.

CHAPTER 3

"WOMAN HERSELF MUST DO THIS WORK": NEW VOICES AND IDEAS FOR WOMEN'S RIGHTS

Like a fire on the horizon, gathering speed and fury as it roared across the earth, the women's rights movement spread in every direction beyond Seneca Falls to distant regions and states. By their words and their courageous examples, women converted one another to the cause of women's rights. Olympia Brown, for example, was still a student at Antioch College in Yellow Springs, Ohio, when she heard Frances Gage, an author and antislavery worker, speak. "It was the first time I had heard a woman preach, and the sense of victory lifted me up." Other women reacted with similar hope and energy, and organized their own activities.

As the women's rights movement gained new converts and leaders, it also developed new ideas. During these early years, women's rights activists decided not to establish a formal organization with officers and bylaws, for fear that, as Angelina Grimké said, an organization would "fetter and distort the expanding mind." They drew most of their support from abolitionists, especially women. They also drew inspiration from the temperance movement, crusades for better schools and healthier ways to live, and spiritualism, a religious movement that aimed to prove the immortality of the soul by making contact with the spirits of the dead. All of these reform

The Una, *published by Paulina Wright Davis, was the first feminist newspaper. In it, Davis voiced her strong support for woman suffrage, women's right to control their reproduction, and their right to be treated as full adults and citizens.*

movements shared the same goal—to improve the way that people lived and help the nation fulfill its democratic ideals.

Despite this shared sense of purpose, however, the women's rights movement had its own goals to pursue, its own tasks to complete. As Elizabeth Cady Stanton had declared at Seneca Falls, "Woman herself must do this work; for woman alone can understand the height, the depth, the length and the breadth of her degradation." The goals that defined the movement before and after the Seneca Falls convention remained the same. Women's rights activists continued to demand all citizenship rights for women. For married women, they demanded control over their own wages, the right to sign legal agreements or contract for property in their own name, stronger inheritance rights after their husbands died, and equal educational and employment opportunities.

But the two central demands were suffrage and a woman's right to determine her own sphere—that is, her goals and aspirations for her life. These demands provoked the most fear and opposition because they challenged traditional notions of women's roles as wife and mother. In reacting to the demand for women's suffrage, one New York State legislator railed, "It is well known that the object of these unsexed women is to overthrow the most sacred of institutions. . . . Are we to put the stamp of truth upon the libel here set forth, that men and women, in the matrimonial relation, are to be equal?"

But women's rights activists did not intend to overthrow the institution of marriage. They accepted marriage and family as important social institutions. They wanted to reform marriage—to elevate the wife's role and therefore equalize her relation to her husband—not abolish it. Indeed, they felt, equality in marriage would lead to happier marriages and a more harmonious family life. Paulina Wright Davis, an activist and editor, argued that a healthy society depended upon a healthy family. "Its evils are the source of all evils, its good the fountain of all good." Reforming marriage was "the starting-point of all the reforms which the world needs."

But women's rights leaders wanted women's sphere to encompass more than marriage and a family. "Woman is too large for the sphere in which society compels her to move," declared Elizabeth Oakes Smith. "Marriage no more fills up the sum of her whole be-

"Family and Fireside," a lithograph published in San Francisco, depicts the domestic bliss that the reformers envisioned. They believed that greater equality between men and women would lead to a more harmonious family life.

ing than it does that of a man." To demonstrate that marriage did not occupy the sum total of their lives, many activists, including Stanton, retained their birth names, adding on their husbands' last names, and preferred not to be called by their husbands' first names. Stanton, for instance, balked at being called "Mrs. *Henry* Stanton" and identified herself as Elizabeth Cady Stanton or simply Mrs. Stanton. Other activists also refused to be called only by their husbands' full names and, once again, drew a parallel to slavery: Only slaves, not free and equal persons, were compelled to take their masters' names and to forfeit their own identity.

Nevertheless, most women's rights activists accepted traditional ideas about women's special maternal qualities and their moral and spiritual superiority, even though they also hoped to enlarge women's opportunities beyond the home. Even Stanton, who decried any limits on women's freedom to live their lives as they wished, extolled women's "high moral sentiments and religious enthusiasms."

It was left to Sojourner Truth, a formidable African-American woman, to define womanhood without relying on traditional images of women. Truth, who had escaped from slavery in New York in 1827, just one year before slavery was abolished in that state,

With her compelling oratory Sojourner Truth demolished the arguments of the opposition to women's rights—that women were inherently weak and frail and needed men's protection, that only intelligent white men deserved equal rights, and that the Bible proclaimed women to be inferior to men.

was born with the first name Isabella. After she rescued one of her children, who had been sold to a planter in Alabama, she worked as a domestic in New York City and joined a religious commune. In 1843, she felt compelled to travel and preach and renamed herself Sojourner Truth.

Truth was a tall, gaunt woman with a regal bearing. At a time when most African-American women were enslaved, she was one of the few black women to play a visible role in the antebellum women's rights movement. At a women's rights convention in Akron, Ohio, in 1851, she mesmerized the crowd with her definition of womanhood. A group of white ministers had tried to monopolize the proceedings by claiming that the Bible prohibited women from participating in any activities beyond the home. Impatient with their views, Truth rose from her seat, amidst gasps and exclamations from the audience, and solemnly walked to the front of the hall.

Cries of "an abolition affair" and "women's rights and niggers!" rang out. Several delegates begged Frances Dana Gage, the president of the convention, to stop Truth from speaking. They warned that "every newspaper in the land will have our cause mixed with abolition and niggers, and we shall be utterly denounced." But Gage ignored these vicious remarks and introduced Sojourner Truth.

Despite the audience's hisses, the tall, dignified Truth began to speak in her deep, rich voice. "That man over there," she said, scornfully referring to one of the ministers, "says that women need to be helped into carriages, and lifted over ditches, and to have the best place everywhere. . . . Nobody ever helps me into carriages, or over mud puddles, or gives me any best place!" She looked her audience straight in the eye. "And a'n't I a woman?"

"Look at me! Look at my arm." She rolled up her right sleeve to expose her strong, muscular arm. "I have plowed, and planted, and gathered into barns, and no man could head me! And a'n't I a woman? I could work as much and eat as much as a man—when I could get it—and bear de lash as well! And a'n't I a woman?"

By now, her audience was spellbound. She continued, "I have borne thirteen children, and seen them most all sold off to slavery. When I cried out with my mother's grief, none but Jesus heard me! And a'n't I a woman?" She then demolished the idea that only educated people deserved equal rights. "If my cup won't hold but a pint, and yours holds a quart, wouldn't you be mean not to let me have my little half-measure full?" She pointed to one of the ministers who had spoken. "Then that little man in black there, he says women can't have as much rights as men, because Christ wasn't a woman! Where did your Christ come from? Where did your Christ come from? From God and a woman! Man had nothing to do with him."

Finally, she warned her audience, "If the first woman God ever made was strong enough to turn the world upside down all alone, these women together ought to be able to turn it back, and get it right side up again! And now they is asking to do it, the men better let them."

As she returned to her seat, the audience erupted into applause. Several spectators sat hushed and still, tears streaming down their cheeks, while others rushed up to shake her hand.

Although few free African-American women participated in the antebellum women's rights movement, they began to challenge inequality within their own communities. In 1848, the same year as the Seneca Falls convention, black women made their first official bid for equality in meetings with black men. At the annual meeting of the National Convention of Colored Freedmen in Cleveland, Ohio, a black woman proposed that women delegates be allowed to speak and vote as equals. Frederick Douglass supported her proposal. After much debate, convention delegates reclassified eligible voters as "persons" instead of men, and allowed women to participate equally.

But despite official decrees to admit women as equal participants, black organizations did not carry out the policy consistently. At state and national conventions, delegates usually scorned women's equal participation and assigned them to such traditional tasks as arranging flowers at delegates' tables while the men determined policy. Even Frederick Douglass, a dedicated advocate of women's rights, put greater priority on ending slavery than achieving female equality within the African-American community and American society.

Other new names and faces joined the cause of women's rights during the 1850s. One of the most dedicated and courageous activists was Susan B. Anthony. Starting in 1851, she and Elizabeth Cady Stanton forged a powerful partnership for women's rights. Born in 1820 in western Massachusetts, Anthony was raised as a Quaker.

When this photograph was taken in 1870, Elizabeth Cady Stanton and Susan B. Anthony had been working together for nearly 20 years. Stanton wrote her colleague, "Our work is one, we are one in aim and sympathy."

Her grandmother and two aunts were influential leaders in the Quaker church, and young Susan B. Anthony was accustomed to hearing women speak their minds.

Her parents also encouraged their daughters to think for themselves and to acquire an education. Daniel Anthony, Susan's father, was an ardent abolitionist, and he urged Susan to devote herself to a social cause. She followed his advice by joining the temperance movement in Rochester, New York, where she quickly rose to become president of the Rochester Daughters of Temperance.

In the spring of 1851, she met Stanton, and the two women hit it off instantly. Stanton immediately recognized Anthony's commitment and skills as a reformer, and Anthony soon became her partner and confidante, someone to whom Stanton could pour out her frustrations at the many domestic obligations which filled her days. "Oh, Susan! Susan! Susan! . . . How much I do long to be free from housekeeping and children, so as to have some time to read and think and write," she wrote Anthony. "But it may be well for me to understand all the trials of woman's lot, that I may more eloquently proclaim them when the time comes."

For the next 50 years the two women worked diligently for women's rights. Later Stanton wrote that she "forged the thunderbolts and [Anthony] fired them." For the first few years, Stanton formulated ideas and wrote speeches, and Anthony supplied the facts, delivered Stanton's speeches, and became a tireless recruiter for new converts to the cause. Anthony's impressive research and organizational skills ably matched Stanton's keen, analytical mind and eloquent pen. Together, they made a powerful team.

Meanwhile, other thinkers and proponents of women's rights also offered a wide array of ideas and initiatives to give women greater autonomy. For a brief period during the early 1850s, the causes of temperance and women's rights became closely linked. Men's addiction to alcohol had a profound impact on women. Wives became impoverished and were physically abused by drunken husbands who had squandered their families' money on alcohol.

Temperance societies not only preached abstinence, they supported legislation to ban alcohol altogether or to prohibit the consumption of alcohol in certain neighborhoods or on certain days of

The temperance crusade took its battle directly to the doors of saloons, where women typically prayed and sang hymns. The temperance movement was closely allied with the drive for women's rights. "Intemperance," wrote one woman's journal, "is the great foe to [woman's] peace and happiness."

The caption for this lithograph identifies Margaret and Catherine Fox and Mrs. Fish as "the original mediums of the mysterious noises at Rochester Western, N.Y." In the 1850s, women spiritualists maintained that their progressive ideas about women's rights were not their own but came instead from the other side.

the week. They also lobbied for laws to protect a wife's property and wages from a husband who would spend her earnings on alcohol. In her 1852 address to the Woman's State Temperance Society convention in Rochester, New York, Stanton boldly urged that drunkenness be made grounds for divorce. "Let no woman remain in the relation of wife with the confirmed drunkard," she declared. "Let no drunkard be the father of her children."

Other women took more direct action: Wielding axes and hatchets, they marched to the saloons in their communities and attacked the buildings. In Marion, Illinois, nine women went on trial for destroying a saloon—and they were defended by a lawyer named Abraham Lincoln.

Besides their close alliance with abolitionists and temperance reformers, women's rights activists received support from an unusual source—mediums and other women who claimed to communicate with the spirit world. In their volume, *The History of Woman Suffrage,* Stanton and Anthony declared, "The only religious sect in the world . . . that has recognized the equality of women is the Spiritualists." The Spiritualist movement began in the same year, 1848, and in the same region, upstate New York, in which the Seneca Falls convention for women's rights was held.

Spiritualism became a popular movement when two young girls, Kate and Margaret Fox, claimed to have made contact with the other side. Within months, other young women had also discovered a talent for contacting the spirit world, and séances were held in parlors throughout the North. Initially, adolescent girls were the most successful mediums. In Ohio in 1852, a student at a girls' school claimed that she and 15 classmates had become mediums. Later on, older women also became mediums.

Like believers in organized religions, such as Christianity and Judaism, Spiritualists claimed that women were pious by nature. But unlike organized religion, Spiritualism thrust women into visible leadership roles and supported the most progressive reform movements of the day. Spiritualists envisioned marriages in which women were equal partners, controlled how many children they wanted, and were free to earn their own wages. Some advocated equal wages for equal work performed by men and women and called for more liberal divorce laws. Others urged women to reject corsets and other confining apparel and wear more comfortable clothes. And most Spiritualists advocated female suffrage. Spiritualists voiced these enlightened views because they believed that women as well as men had the ability to grasp truths without the guidance of a religious authority such as a minister or rabbi. But, they claimed, unjust laws and social customs had denied women the opportunity to develop their full potential as citizens and human beings capable of comprehending moral and religious truths.

Besides working for legal and political rights, activists also devised bold and original proposals to improve the health and personal well-being of women. Paulina Wright Davis, for example, urged women to be more knowledgeable about their anatomy and reproduction. Even physicians were loath to discuss such "indelicate" matters with their female patients, or they simply assumed that women had far less sexual desire than men. To combat the ignorance surrounding women's physiology and sexuality, Davis gave public lectures, using a plaster figure of a female nude. Some of her more delicate listeners, however, were shocked by such a display, and either covered their eyes, fled from the room, or fainted.

In 1853, Davis also founded one of the first journals devoted to women's rights, the *Una*. The title is the feminine form of the Latin word meaning *one*. In her columns, she urged women to demand the right to limit the number of children they bore and to take control over men's sexual access to them. She wanted women to enjoy the full rights and privileges of adulthood. "We ask to be regarded, respected, and treated as human beings, of full age and natural abilities," she wrote in the *Una,* "as equal fellow sinners, and not as infants or beautiful angels, to whom the rules of civil and social justice do not apply."

Stanton also fought for women's personal freedom, especially in the sexual relations between husbands and wives. She endorsed, in her words, "the right of a wife to her own person"—that is, a wife's right to refuse sexual intercourse with her husband, especially if she did not want to have more children. In 1853, Stanton lamented that many women did not yet have this right. "Man in his lust has regulated long enough this whole question of sexual intercourse," she wrote to Anthony. "Now let the mothers of mankind . . . set bounds to his indulgence."

Paulina Wright Davis, an early and ardent proponent of women's rights, once said she was not truly happy until she "felt free to think and act from my own convictions."

By the early 1850s, a few forms of birth control were available to women, notably the douche and different types of intrauterine devices. Women were also familiar with the rhythm method, in which they had intercourse only during the time of the month when they believed that they were not fertile. But ignorance about the female fertility cycle diminished the effectiveness of this form of birth control.

Women also resorted to abortion, although abortions were beyond the means of many women. In 1858, the price of an abortion ranged from $25 to $60, an exorbitant price for a working woman barely able to make ends meet on a salary of $3 or $4 a week. In addition, abortions could be dangerous when performed by a quack, and were increasingly frowned upon by traditionally minded physicians for moral as well as medical reasons. As states began to make the practice of abortion a crime, women were less able to secure a safe, medically sound abortion, and resorted to using painful and dangerous homemade devices.

Even women who disagreed with many of the tenets of the women's

The hotel and mineral springs in Stafford, Connecticut, near Hartford, was the nation's first health spa. Women found at such water-cure establishments a sympathetic female community among other patrons and staff members and a welcome alternative to mainstream medicine.

rights movement sought ways to improve the quality of women's lives. Catharine Beecher opposed female suffrage and believed that women's greatest contribution lay in being mothers, wives, homemakers, and teachers. To her way of thinking, these social roles tapped women's special maternal qualities. Unlike Stanton and others, she did not crusade to break down all social and legal barriers to women's advancement. Instead, throughout the 1830s and 1840s she focused her energies on investing women's homemaking duties with greater power and dignity. She believed that healthy, happy homes—created by women—led to a healthy, happy society.

Calisthenics were one answer for women who found it hard to get enough exercise. Harper's Weekly *complained that "the employments of American women, especially of those resident in cities, are so entirely sedentary, that they do continual violence to the laws of nature."*

But if Beecher was not ready for women to become doctors or lawyers or politicians, she wanted them to be physically well and able. She was a leading proponent of water cures. From the 1840s to the 1880s, water-cure centers sprang up around the North and Midwest and catered primarily to women, who stayed at these cure centers for several days or weeks. There, they followed a regimen of bathing, using wet compresses, taking steam baths and massages, and exercising. They also drank cold water and followed rigorous diets, and they learned about new forms of birth control.

Water cures brought women together to share the pleasures of indulging in healthful physical activities. While mainstream physicians preached to women about the incurable pain associated with the monthly menses and childbirth—a pain that women were predestined to suffer because of the biblical Eve's disobedience of divine commandments, they claimed—water cures helped women ease ailments and diseases that were connected with the female reproductive system.

Beecher also exhorted women to get adequate exercise and fresh air, eat nourishing meals, and stop wearing tight-fitting corsets, which endangered women's internal organs. Like Paulina Wright Davis, she urged women to learn about their bodies—in large part to protect their sexual virtue. Beecher believed that knowledge was the most potent weapon against sexual promiscuity. In 1855, she published her views in *Letters to the People on Health and Happiness.* Beecher was not prepared to challenge existing social and political distinctions between men and women. But she was a forceful, energetic advocate for giving women greater control over their physical health and well-being.

Godey's Lady's Book, *a popular 19th-century magazine, showed the latest fashions: dresses with constricting corsets and many heavy layers of petticoats.*

Efforts to reform women's clothing also aimed to give women greater physical comfort and freedom of movement. Tightly corseted dresses with their layers and layers of petticoats, which most women wore, could weigh up to 12 pounds, and the rigid steel and whalebone corsets prevented easy movement and breathing. These fashions were definitely not made for comfort. Nor were they safe. Not only did the corsets constrict women's ability to breathe comfortably, but they could easily trip over the long, full skirts, especially when they walked up stairs. Before the days of electricity, a woman often had to climb the steps holding a candle or oil lamp in one hand and perhaps a baby in the other. With no hand free to hold up the layers of petticoat and skirt, she could easily catch a foot in the skirt, injuring herself and the baby, and set the place on fire.

Among the new ideas for women's apparel were bloomers, a costume composed of a loose-fitting skirt that came below the knees and was worn over pantaloons. The pantaloons ballooned out and gathered at each ankle with a short ruffle. When Elizabeth Smith Miller, Stanton's cousin, introduced pantaloons to America after discovering them in Europe, they caused a minor sensation, especially among Stanton and other women who recognized their comfort. The new garment became known as bloomers after editor and temperance advocate Amelia Bloomer described them in the *Lily,* a magazine for women. Within days, hundreds of women deluged the paper with requests for more information about the costume, and Bloomer published sewing instructions. But many people ridiculed women who wore this unorthodox garment.

Beyond the controversy over bloomers, women's rights activists faced intense opposition for daring to want greater social and political equality for women. In 1854, Susan Anthony selected 60 women to circulate petitions throughout New York State demanding suffrage and equal economic and legal rights for wives. For 10 weeks during the middle of winter, Anthony and her recruits canvassed the state, holding meetings and going door to door to collect signatures. They all had trouble finding adequate lodgings and being seated in restaurants because innkeepers frowned upon women traveling without a male escort. But the hardest part was having doors slammed in their faces by men—and women—who disapproved of their work. To these opponents and others, any form of female assertion conjured up images of women stepping out of their rightful domestic sphere and invading the male domain of commerce and politics.

Stanton's father even threatened to erase her name from his will if she insisted on addressing the New York legislature. Stanton was outraged. "I passed through a terrible scourging when last at my father's," she wrote to Anthony. "I cannot tell you how deeply the iron entered my soul. I never felt more keenly the degradation of my sex. To think that all in me of which my father would have felt a proper pride had I been a man, is deeply mortifying to him because I am a woman. That thought has stung me to a fierce decision—to speak as soon as I can do myself credit. . . . Sometimes, Susan, I struggle in deep waters." Stanton continued to speak in public, though infrequently, and remained in her father's will when he died in 1859.

For every ounce of comfort it gave, the bloomer outfit also provoked sneers and derision. Clergymen condemned the costume because it violated the biblical commandment that men and women must not wear the same garments. Some men and boys even threw rocks and eggs at women who wore bloomers in public.

By 1857, women's rights activists faced one other obstacle to achieving their goals—the growing crisis over slavery. Mounting tension between the North and South brought the nation ominously close to Civil War. In 1857, the infamous *Dred Scott* decision alarmed abolitionists and delighted slaveholders. The U.S. Supreme Court ruled that slaves remained in bondage even when they were taken by their masters, or had escaped, to free states.

This decision opened up the possibility that slavery could not be restricted to the southern slaveholding states, because slave owners

In the case of the slave Dred Scott, Chief Justice Roger Taney ruled that blacks could not be citizens. On the contrary, they were "a subordinate and inferior class of beings, and whether emancipated or not ... had no rights or privileges but such as those who held the power and the Government might choose to grant them."

could take their property—their slaves—to nonslaveholding territories and states, where they could continue to practice slavery. Abolitionists feared that the Supreme Court might declare that all states—including nonslaveholding states—could no longer exclude slavery, because that would violate the 5th Amendment's protection of the slave owner's rights to property, including human property.

As a result, Lucy Stone Blackwell, Antoinette Brown Blackwell, and other women's rights activists shifted their attention from women's rights to abolition. Women's rights leaders canceled their 1857 annual convention because of a lack of money and followers. Stanton and Anthony despaired that all they had worked for was coming apart.

By the eve of the Civil War, however, the movement had achieved one significant victory: passage of an amendment to the New York State 1848 Married Woman's Property Act. This amendment gave women the right to keep their own earnings and invest any money or transact any business in their own name without their husbands' permission or involvement. They could also keep any property inherited or received as a gift. In addition, women could sign contracts and instigate lawsuits.

This law was a major victory for married women. It took them out of the legal and economic category of "children, idiots, and lunatics," as previous statutes had classified them, and helped to abolish the notion of women's "legal death" in marriage. Next to suffrage, which women would not achieve for another 60 years, this law was a major milestone in American women's quest for autonomy. By 1860, other states, including Indiana, Maine, Missouri, and Ohio, had also passed laws to allow married women to keep their own earnings.

That same year, at the Tenth National Women's Rights Convention, Stanton introduced 10 resolutions favoring more liberal divorce laws. Only Anthony and a handful of others supported her. The delegates voted, and the issue was tabled and recorded—that is, acknowledged in the record but not acted upon. At that time, women in New York State were entitled to sue for divorce only on grounds of adultery. A few other states also allowed women to sue for divorce on the grounds of the husband's desertion or failure to provide for his wife and children. Stanton urged that marriages be

At the Woman's Rights Convention in 1859 in New York City, the speakers provoked spirited responses from both the men and women attending.

treated as a simple contract that could be quickly and quietly dissolved on the grounds of drunkenness, insanity, desertion, brutality, adultery, or incompatibility. Despite hostile public reaction, Stanton continued to believe that more liberal divorce laws were essential for giving women greater freedom and protection in marriage.

With the nation hurtling toward Civil War, women's rights activists now shifted their energies to wartime concerns. The battle for suffrage, for divorce reform and women's control over reproduction, for greater educational and employment opportunities, and for more comfortable and healthful clothing would have to wait while the nation fought a terrible civil war. But in these prewar years, the women's rights movement had set the stage for further battles—and some victories—in the crusade to make women equal citizens and human beings in their own right, separate from their husbands and fathers, sons and brothers. A chorus of new ideas about women's lives had been raised, and the strong, supple voices of reform would not be silenced.

CHAPTER 4

"THE 'EL DORADO' OF OUR HOPES": JOURNEYS TO NEW PLACES

Like the Pilgrims who journeyed to the New World more than two centuries earlier, people flocked to America throughout the first half of the 19th century to seek a better life. At the same time, thousands of Americans journeyed to uncharted regions within the country for new opportunities. But unlike the Pilgrims, who fled from religious persecution, these new migrants searched mostly for better economic opportunities.

They came from the small towns and cities of the eastern region of the United States to the gold-laden hills of California, and from the centuries-old farms and cities of Europe to the burgeoning young cities of the Northeast and the prairie grasslands of the Midwest. By ship and wagon train, by rail and carriage, they swarmed over the American landscape.

White settlers had been pushing back the western boundaries of the United States since the earliest days of the young republic. In 1803, after dispatching two explorers to survey the region, President Thomas Jefferson purchased the Louisiana Territory, the expanse of land extending west from the Mississippi River to the Rocky Mountains and north from the Gulf of Mexico to the border of Canada. With this purchase, the United States doubled its size, and fertile new farm and grasslands became available for settlement.

A wagon train threads its way over the rugged terrain. The journey out West could seem endless. One traveler confided in her diary: "I am very weary of this journey, weary of myself and all around me. I long for the quiet of home where I can be at peace once more."

When miners journeyed to California in the late 1840s in search of gold, some took their wives and children.

As settlers pushed farther west, beckoned by the promise of new land for crops and livestock and new opportunities for commerce, they wrote glowing letters to friends and family back home. "We had heard so much of the beautiful prairies of Iowa," a young girl from Pennsylvania wrote in the 1840s. "We could see for miles and all my longings for the vast open spaces were satisfied."

Starting in the 1840s, Americans believed that their nation was destined to expand all the way west to the Pacific Ocean. Their eyes lit up at the prospect of the abundant land and natural resources awaiting development, and they were eager to spread the ideas of democracy and Christianity to native peoples—who already had their own highly developed cultures.

This belief in what Americans called "manifest destiny"—the steady, inevitable expansion of the nation all the way to the Pacific shores—propelled the U.S. government in 1845 to annex the Republic of Texas, which had recently won its independence from Mexico, and to foment a bloody war with Mexico in 1846 to capture more territory. When Mexico surrendered in 1848, the United States acquired the sprawling expanse of what is now California, Nevada, Utah, Arizona, and part of Colorado and New Mexico.

Unbeknownst until the discovery of gold in California in 1848, the country also gained a treasure trove of precious minerals. The brilliant sparkle of those golden ores flashed as far away as the hills and valleys of New England, and gold seekers eager for instant riches immediately set out for California.

The gold rushers who went to California were mostly men, but soon more families began to migrate west for new economic opportunities. From 1850 to 1852, the number of families who went west surged. In 1852, a correspondent for the *Daily Missouri Republican* observed, "A marked feature of the emigration this year is the number of women who are going out by the land route." Indeed, families stood a better chance of acquiring more land than single people. In Oregon, the Donation Land Act of 1850 granted families twice the amount of land that single men received.

Both single and married women made the journey. Throughout the 1840s, educator and writer Catharine Beecher trained and dispatched hundreds of single, young female teachers to open schools

Many women gave birth along the trail, but the real challenge came in keeping infants clean and dry. Water for washing diapers was scarce, and mothers often reused soiled diapers by merely drying, scraping, and airing them.

in frontier regions. There they lived among pioneer families, boarding for a time with each family in the new community.

Some homesteading wives reluctantly went along with their more enthusiastic husbands, dreading the hardships and uncertainty that lay ahead. In 1853, before heading west from Kansas to Oregon, Elizabeth Goltra mournfully wrote in her diary, "I am leaving my home, my early friends and associates never to see them again, exchanging the disinterested solicitude of fond friends for the cold and unsympathetic friendship of strangers." She continued, "Shall we all reach the 'El Dorado' of our hopes or shall one of our number be left and our graves be in the dreary wilderness?"

Other women, however, were as eager as their husbands, sharing their hopes for a better life. "Ho—for California—at last we are on the way," an excited Helen Carpenter wrote in her diary in 1857, "and with good luck may some day reach the 'promised land.'"

The excitement of heading for this promised land did not ease the hardships along the way. Travelers had to be prepared for changing weather and terrain, and they also lived with the ever-present fear of attacks by Indian tribes angered by this invasion of their ancestral lands. When Mary Jane Caples met a group of Pawnees during her journey to California in 1849, she was overcome by fear. "They were the first Indians I had ever seen," she recalled later, "and to my frightened vision . . . they looked ten feet high—my thought was that they would kill us all, and take my baby in captivity."

On the trail, women performed many of the same duties they had done back home—cooking, washing, and caring for their children. But the conditions under which they worked were far more primitive. They had to convert the small space of a tent or wagon bed into a temporary home, stretch out limited amounts of water for cooking and cleaning, cook outdoors over an open fire while fighting dust and insects, and make tasty meals with a minimum of ingredients. As Helen Carpenter ruefully noted in her diary, "One does like a change and about the only change we have from bread and bacon is to bacon and bread." Women gathered wild fruits and berries along the way to bake into pies and tarts to add variety to their families' diets.

Yet there were moments of relief from these burdens. Crossing the Great Plains or the desert could be monotonous after endless

A westward-bound caravan assembles for the day's journey. The long, dusty days, arduous trail chores, and crowded living conditions tested the patience of even the most adventurous woman.

days of unchanging landscape—or it could be a magical journey into a mysterious new land. As she crossed the Plains to California in 1860, Lavinia Porter could not get over the sheer "beauty . . . surrounding us on all sides." She exclaimed, "The air was filled with a balmy sweetness, and yet so limpid and clear that even in the starlight we could catch glimpses of the shimmering trees in the distant river."

On the trail, women spent some of their most pleasurable moments in each other's company—around a campfire at night, knitting and talking over the day's events, cooking, or washing together. Catherine Haun, who crossed the Plains in 1849, recalled, "During the day, we womenfolk visited from wagon to wagon or congenial friends spent an hour walking, ever westward, and talking over our home life back in 'the states' . . . voicing our hopes for the future and even whispering a little friendly gossip of emigrant life."

Finally, after the long days on the trail, after endless hours of wondering what their new homes would look like, travelers arrived at their destinations—only to discover more hardship ahead. Even the hardiest woman was brought down by the sight of her new home—a crude log cabin without doors or windows; a shack with tar paper walls, canvas ceiling, and a dirt floor; or a dirty brown soddie—a dwelling made out of hard-packed soil—which often housed insects

Cooking, cleaning, and child care were not much easier in frontier homes than on the trail. Dust seeped through cracks in the wall and covered everything, and women continued to cook with limited equipment.

and snakes in its four walls. Many settlers had no home at all until the family built one. Mary Rabb spent her first weeks in Texas "spinning under a tree," with only "a quilt and a sheat [sic] for a tent."

But women made do. Just as they did on the trails, they set up homemaking in their new dwellings. They tried to make their homes cheerful and cozy by arranging the few treasured possessions they had brought from home and covering the walls with newspaper, muslin, even geological maps as decoration. Many dwellings became very homey.

Hannah Anderson Ropes, a black woman who settled in Kansas in 1855, wrote to her mother in Massachusetts that she hoped to establish a "proper" home in her new surroundings. She reported that she hung "Bay State Shawls" on her cabin walls like tapestries and displayed her "choice China" as decoration. "How we begin to look forward to a condition of civilized housekeeping!" she declared.

While the men cleared the fields for farming, or panned for gold and silver, women did the work of homemaking. They cooked and cleaned, baked bread and pies, sewed their families' clothing, preserved foodstuffs for the winter, made soap and candles, and raised chickens and vegetables. Because of the spartan conditions under which they worked, they took special pride in a well-made pair of trousers or a good meal.

Women also shared the hard, physical labor with their husbands. They helped construct homes, drove plows, sawed and hauled timber, and stood guard at night for fires or predators. As one Oklahoma woman recalled, "In those days the wife had to help do everything."

Still, women were primarily responsible for the essential work of homemaking. They even turned some domestic tasks into an opportunity to relax and socialize. Quilting parties, for example, were a favorite pastime in which women visited together while working on a quilt. For some, the process of making a quilt symbolized their new lives on the frontier. As one woman homesteader in Kentucky recalled, "You see you start out with just so much [calico]; . . . the neighbors will give you a piece here and a piece there, and you will have a piece left every time you cut out a dress, and you take what happens to come and that's predestination . . . and that is just the way with livin'. The Lord sends in the pieces, but we can cut 'em and put 'em together pretty much to suit ourselves."

Black women had less opportunity to attend quilting parties and other social events because few other blacks lived nearby. Both black

Churning butter was a major occupation in the late summer and early fall, as women worked together to lay in a winter's supply. It was also an occasion for women to enjoy each other's company.

A folk artist's view of a quilting party in which both men and women participated. While the women were busy sewing, the men watched the children.

and white women settlers experienced the painful loneliness and physical hardships of living on the frontier. But black women felt even more isolated because of their small numbers and because most whites did not want to live and work with them. Some whites—even those who opposed slavery—did not want to compete against blacks for land and work, and they supported efforts to restrict blacks from migrating or purchasing land. In Iowa, free blacks were required to show a certificate of freedom before being allowed to settle, and most western states and territories in the 1850s and 1860s prohibited black inhabitants from testifying against whites in court or from riding stagecoaches and streetcars. Black and white settlers alike shared the hardships of homesteading, but rarely did these shared difficulties blossom into mutual support or friendship.

Throughout the frontier, from the lush green valleys of Oregon to the flat, arid lands of the desert Southwest, both black and white women settlers used their talents and resources to help their families and communities. A higher percentage of free black women worked outside of their homes because of economic necessity. Most black women worked as domestics, while others became washerwomen, cooks, dressmakers, and nursemaids. Like black domestics and laundresses back home, they toiled long hours for meager wages and endured their employers' demeaning treatment. But on the frontier, they worked under far more primitive conditions. A small number of black women also ran boardinghouses or taught black schoolchildren.

White women worked by preparing meals for single men in the community or selling home-baked bread and pies. They also sold cloth they had spun, made shirts and trousers for sale, or took in laundry. Women who had extra room also took in boarders. Other women worked as cooks, waitresses, and chambermaids in inns and boardinghouses, or opened their own boardinghouses or taverns.

Educated white women became columnists for the "Ladies' Department" of western newspapers or wrote novels about life on the frontier. From 1854 to 1857, Elizabeth Barstow Stoddard wrote as "our Lady Correspondent" for the San Francisco daily *Alta California*. And women taught, both in frontier schools and in mission schools set up by religious orders to educate and convert Native American children. Women also pursued less genteel professions, such as prostitution and brothel-keeping.

As they put their cabins and shanties in order, women also tried to bring order to their new communities. Like their urban sisters back home, both black and white women settlers organized schools, churches, and clubs in their frontier communities. These various institutions were segregated by race, and far fewer community groups existed among black settlers because of their small numbers. Until homesteaders could afford to build a school or church, they conducted prayer meetings and schools in their own tiny dwellings. Women

A woman at a California gold mining camp, 1852. Life in these frontier outposts was harsh and lawless because of "the want of respectable female society," according to one miner. This camp, however, seems an exception.

This portrait of Tulares Feather and her child appeared in a book on California by a British visitor. Armed conflict, disease, famine, and forced resettlement gradually destroyed the communal, agrarian way of life that Native Americans had known for centuries. Indian mothers bore primary responsibility for transmitting the traditions of their agrarian culture to their children, who, from an early age, helped their mothers tend crops and gather berries or nuts.

sponsored box suppers, theatricals, and other events to raise money for a school building and teacher. They also organized and taught Sunday schools, planned church socials, and participated in missionary societies.

In time, homesteading women organized other social activities, such as reading clubs, literary and debating societies, and amateur musical and dramatic groups. Women's charitable groups also sprang up to assist widows, care for orphaned children, and distribute Bibles among local Native American populations. Women strove to bring civility and morality to their own communities by decrying the gambling, drinking, and general lawlessness that men had introduced to the frontier. Julia Lovejoy, a migrant to Kansas in the 1850s, lamented that in Kansas City the "inhabitants and the morals, are of an indescribably repulsive and undesirable character."

Lovejoy and other homesteaders who hoped to civilize the western regions pointed to the wilderness itself as the cause of the "undesirable character" of many of its inhabitants. Although they admired its natural beauty and abundant resources, the wilderness also represented godlessness and the dark, mysterious aspects of existence. At the center of this frightful setting, to their way of thinking, stood Native Americans, who had lived in the western regions for centuries, wresting their livelihoods and cultural and spiritual traditions from the land.

Most settlers did not understand or respect the Native Americans' way of life, a life dependent upon the bounty of the earth. While Native American men hunted game, women collected seeds and roots and harvested crops. Native Americans looked to the sky and the soil for spiritual sustenance as well. The natural world embodied their deities, and their religious traditions and folkways expressed a gentle, respectful love of the earth and all things natural—a reverence that homesteaders who wanted to exploit the land for commercial gain did not share.

By the 1840s and 1850s, homesteaders crossing overland began to encounter large numbers of Native Americans. In Iowa and Kansas, homesteaders came upon Pawnees and Winnebagos. The Sioux predominated in the Great Plains and Minnesota, while the Cheyenne tribes made their homes in Wyoming, Montana, Colorado, and Kansas. Apache tribes inhabited the dry, arid desert lands of Texas, and both Apaches and Pueblo tribes lived in New Mexico. Farther west, the Nez Percés populated the Blue Mountains of Oregon. Other tribes also inhabited the western lands. For centuries, until the first white settlers encroached upon their lands, these tribes coexisted with each other, sometimes peacefully, sometimes warily, farming the land and hunting great herds of buffalo, whose bodies they used for meat, clothing, and shelter.

Lurid accounts of Indian attacks filled white children's schoolbooks and the novels their parents read, and fed homesteaders' fears and prejudices against Indians. As the homesteaders came into contact with Native Americans in towns and camps where they stopped to replenish supplies, their fears gradually gave way to a mixture of curiosity and contempt. Harriet Bishop, a missionary who taught in a Minnesota mission school in the 1840s, described the Native Americans she met as "disgustingly filthy," "extremely unchaste" in their manner of dress, and "imbedded in moral pollution." Missionary and nonmissionary women alike regarded the religious beliefs and practices of Native Americans as inferior to their own. "The Indians' ideas of the creation of the world were ludicrous and absurd," Mary Sagatoo, another missionary, wrote. "As a race they are . . . without power of mind or hand to record truthfully events as they occur."

A white girl loses her legs to the knife of an Indian woman during the Minnesota Massacre of 1862. The girl's mother, at left, watches helplessly.

But friendships between Native Americans and homesteaders occasionally flourished. Sometimes they traded foodstuffs and supplies, such as Native American baskets or moccasins for flour, sugar, or coffee. And sometimes neighboring Indians generously supplied fish, game, and wild fruits and berries to homesteaders living on scanty diets. Southwestern tribes taught homesteaders how to build adobe dwellings, and elsewhere Native American neighbors helped settlers find temporary shelter. During the Civil War, a group of Arkansas women fleeing from oncoming Union troops took shelter with a Cherokee family. Native Americans also hired themselves out as domestics, ranch and farm hands, and nursemaids for settlers' children.

But these rare, fragile instances of goodwill between Native Americans and homesteaders could not repair the profound sense of loss and displacement that Native Americans endured as settlers moved in on their ancestral and farming lands and wantonly destroyed the land and game that had sustained them. Between 1845 and 1860, in California alone, 115,000 Native Americans died from disease, malnutrition, and murder as homesteaders and gold rushers moved in on their land.

Native Americans and settlers engaged in bloody conflicts, and innocent people on both sides were massacred. As white settlers advanced, claiming Indian tribal lands as their own and breaking the terms of treaties they had signed, Native Americans tried to defend their land. In the 1850s, Pacific Northwestern tribes rose up to defend their homes, and in Minnesota the Sioux fought mightily against oncoming settlers. Cheyenne and Arapaho tribes in Colorado raided settlements to drive homesteaders away. In Apache tribes, some women joined their men on the battleground, while others served as messengers and emissaries between Apache warriors and U.S. military officers.

Native American women shared their brethren's contempt for the way that white settlers plundered the land and mocked their centuries-old traditions. And just as white women feared assault by Native American men, Indian women had far greater reason to fear white men, who freely raped them or forced them into marriages.

Armed conflict, disease, famine, and forced resettlement gradually destroyed the communal, agrarian way of life that Native Ameri-

A huge stream of immigrants from Europe arrives in New York Harbor to begin a new life. They viewed the United States as a land of opportunity—because they took the jobs that no one else wanted.

cans had known for centuries. The Promised Land of opportunity to which homesteaders flocked—the land that Native Americans had cultivated and venerated for so long—became a trail of tears watered by the bloodshed and anguish of native peoples driven from their homeland.

While homesteaders streamed across the American landscape to settle the western regions, another hardy group of migrants journeyed across the Atlantic Ocean to America. Like the homesteaders, they came to seek a better way of life. And they, too, endured a hard, long journey. But they did not see a changing landscape or stop to pick wildflowers along the way. Their only scenery was endless miles of water, or the filthy, airless rooms below deck where they ate and slept. Sometimes the ocean was a placid place to be and sometimes it was terrifying, especially during a storm. Elise Isely, an immigrant from Switzerland who came to the United States in 1855, described how her ship tossed and turned during a storm like a toy boat. "Salt water was spurted in. . . . The breaking waves boomed like never-ending thunder."

Once they landed, immigrants had to be wary of swindlers and thieves eager to trick them out of their money and possessions. Sometimes local hotels and boardinghouses hired "runners," who "greeted" immigrants at the docks by grabbing their baggage and demanding

2

Irish peasants gather hopefully at the port of Cork to leave for America. Upon arriving in their new country, Irish immigrant women found that they were in great demand as domestics and as mill and factory hands. But the wages were meager and the hours long.

that they follow them to nearby lodgings. If the immigrants did not want to lose their bags, they had no choice but to follow obligingly. In 1855, New York City, the major port of entry, built facilities in lower Manhattan to process immigrants and their possessions in an orderly manner and provide them with information on how to meet family members and travel to inland destinations. As a result, swindlers had a harder time taking advantage of newcomers.

In 1840, 84,000 immigrants entered the United States. Ten years later, in 1850, 369,000 immigrants came to America. Between 1840 and 1860, approximately 4.2 million newcomers journeyed to the United States. About 40 percent of them were Irish refugees escaping a devastating famine in Ireland. For years, potatoes had been the staple food of the Irish. But in 1845, a terrible blight wiped out Ireland's potato crop. Millions of people went hungry or lost their chief occupation—potato farming. Between 1847 and 1854, the worst years of the famine, more than 1.25 million people fled Ireland to the United States, hoping to find work. Many of the Irish immigrants were single young women forced to support themselves. Immigrants from Germany, Norway, Sweden, Scotland, Wales, and England also came to the United States.

Most immigrants came over simply to make more money. Many, such as the Irish, remained in this country, but other immigrants stayed long enough to earn a substantial amount of money and then returned to their homelands. Most immigrants settled in towns and cities, especially New York and Boston. But some journeyed to the West to start a farm or small business. Colonies of German immigrants headed for Texas in the 1840s and Wisconsin in the 1850s, while Swedes and Norwegians settled in large numbers in Minnesota, Iowa, North and South Dakota, Wisconsin, and Nebraska. Except for the Irish, who for the most part avoided rural life and settled in industrial towns and cities in the North and Midwest, immigrants from other ethnic backgrounds fanned across the American landscape, as far west as California and Oregon. Wherever they settled, in cities or out on the frontier, they sought out family, friends, and other newcomers from back home. They wanted to live among their own.

Newcomers were astonished by the abundance of food and the higher standard of living among Americans in general. Jannicke Saehle, a young Norwegian woman who came to Wisconsin alone, wrote home about the many tasty dishes she ate in her new homeland. "My greatest regret here is to see the superabundance of food, much of which has to be thrown to the chickens and the swine, when I think of my dear ones in Bergen, who like so many others must at this time lack the necessities of life." Immigrants also discovered new food in America. They marveled over wild raspberries, strawberries, and asparagus, and stumbled upon watermelons, a fruit they did not have back home, "as big as a child's head."

Like American-born homesteaders, immigrant homesteaders also flinched at the untamed features of the western region. Elisabeth Koren, from Norway, cried out in her diary, "This is really too much! . . . A snake in the house! . . . It was probably one of those harmless grass snakes, but it was at least two feet long, and it is horrid that such visitors can get into the house."

More worrisome, however, especially for immigrants who lived in towns and cities, was the prejudice of Americans who feared or disliked people different from themselves. Many Americans wanted to reduce the political power of foreign-born voters by extending the waiting period from 5 to 21 years before immigrants became

A family of poor Irish immigrants in New York City huddles together in this somewhat sentimental depiction of their situation.

eligible for American citizenship and voting rights. In some states, some people wanted to prevent any foreign-born citizens from holding public office. By restricting immigrants' voting rights and political power, they hoped to discourage immigration to the United States, especially by the Irish, the immigrant group whom they most despised.

As more Irish immigrants poured into the country, anti-Irish sentiment grew even more intense. When Americans referred to Irish neighbors or employees, they used such belittling nicknames as "Bridget" or "Paddy." Irish men and women seeking work in American towns and cities encountered signs declaring "No Irish Need Apply." In 1860, an Irish immigrant who had worked on the railroads poured out his frustration in a letter back home: "It would take more than a mere letter to tell you the despicable, humiliating, slavish life of an Irish laborer on a railroad in the States; . . . everything . . . is against him; no love for him—no protection in life; can be shot down, run through, kicked, cuffed, spat on; and no redress."

Other immigrants besides the Irish endured similar prejudice. Many factories refused to hire any immigrants and those that did assigned them to the lowest paying, least skilled, and most dangerous work. But for immigrants desperate to work, these obstacles were not insurmountable. And America offered most of them more economic opportunities, a higher standard of living, and more independence than they had known in the countries they had left.

Irish women, for example, were expected to be economically independent at an early age and to contribute to their families' upkeep. Thousands of single young Irish women came to America to work, make a new life for themselves, and send money home to their families. And, indeed, they sent most of the millions of dollars that flowed from America to Ireland during the 1840s and 1850s. They prided themselves on their ability to learn new skills and earn money.

Single Irish women fared better in America than married or widowed Irish women. A husband's desertion or death usually rendered a married woman penniless. But a single Irish woman could always find work as a live-in domestic. A married woman with children had no such choice. She needed to earn enough money to support both herself and her children, and few women had the skills to do so. More than any other destitute women, widowed or abandoned Irish women relied on some form of charitable assistance.

In 1843, an order of nuns, the Sisters of Mercy, settled in Pittsburgh, Pennsylvania, and opened a Mercy House, where women in need could find refuge. Soon, they opened Mercy Houses in other major cities, including New York, Chicago, Baltimore, San Francisco, St. Louis, and Philadelphia. They also established training programs in nursing and clerical work, employment agencies, boardinghouses, and day nurseries for the children of working mothers. The Sisters of Mercy offered their services to any women in need, Irish and non-Irish. But Irish women were their most numerous recipients.

Whether migrants came from the Old World to the New or from the towns and cities of one side of America to the other, all migrants harbored bright hopes for a better way of life for themselves and their families. Some migrants never completed the journey. They died along the way, either on the boats navigating the Atlantic Ocean or on the dusty overland trails. And some regretted having made the journey once they had reached their final destinations. But other migrants fought off the powerful waves of homesickness and regret that occasionally washed over them and eagerly applied themselves to their new lives. The words of one anonymous Norwegian immigrant woman perhaps expressed the thoughts of thousands of other migrants: "When I think, however, that there will be a better livelihood for us here than in poor Norway, I reconcile myself to it and thank God, who protected me and mine over the ocean's waves and led us to a fruitful land."

CHAPTER 5

"I HAVE REACHED THE AGE FOR ACTION": WOMEN SEARCH FOR A VOCATION

In the mid-19th century, a young woman's 18th birthday marked a milestone—a rite of passage from childhood and the strong hand of parental authority to the sober concerns of adulthood. At 18, women came of legal age. If unmarried, they were entitled to keep any property or earnings they acquired, and they could marry without their parents' permission. Beyond that, they possessed no rights as citizens. Like their mothers and other older women, they could not vote or serve on a jury. In practice, coming of legal age mainly freed young women from parental authority, though many daughters who worked continued to contribute their wages to their families or helped their parents in other ways.

Still, for some women, turning 18 marked a divide in their lives, a chance to make their own decisions and determine how to spend their adult years, within the limited number of choices available to them. Frances Willard, a future social reformer, used the opportunity of turning 18 to read a novel that her parents had earlier forbidden her to read. When her father scolded her, she reminded him, as she recalled later, that "I am 18—I am of age—I am now to do what I think right, and to read this fine historical story [*Ivanhoe* by Sir Walter Scott] is, in my opinion, a right thing for me to do."

All of the women graduates of Oberlin College, class of 1855, along with the principal and a member of the Ladies' Board sat for a commemorative daguerreotype. The three women in the left of the front row graduated from the regular college department but were nonetheless supervised by the Ladies' Department, which had a more traditional curriculum.

Emma Willard, the founder of Troy Female Seminary, advocated a rigorous education for women. She believed that the nation itself would benefit from educating its women: "Who knows how great and good a race of men may yet arise from the forming hand of mothers enlightened?"

But this exhilirating sense of freedom was overshadowed by a painful awareness of how limited freedom was for women. They watched brothers choose from among a variety of colleges and vocations that were closed to them or, in later years, go off to vote for the first time. When Frances Willard's brother went to vote, Willard turned to her sister, Mary, and tearfully asked, "Wouldn't you like to vote as well as Oliver? Don't you and I love the country just as well as he, and doesn't the country need our ballots?"

For young women who had completed their schooling and who did not marry or were not already working, graduation posed a big question mark as they pondered their next step. Willard, for example, later described the two years following graduation as "often very dull and sometimes very gay" but also "the most difficult" in her life because she had not yet found her "vocation." She felt adrift, without direction or purpose. "I remember that I used to think myself smart. I used to plan great things that I would do and be. . . . But it is over. The mist has cleared away and I dream no longer, though I am only twenty-one years old." In fact, Willard did find her vocation, though not right away. She eventually became a teacher and, in later years, the president of the Woman's Christian Temperance Union (WCTU), an organization opposed to alcohol consumption. Under her leadership, the WCTU developed an ambitious program of social reform to improve all aspects of women's lives.

Willard was one of many middle-class young women who bemoaned their seeming lack of purpose after graduation. At 25, Emily Blackwell confided in her journal that she had "reached the age for action, for great deeds and what is accomplished? How terrible it must be to look back upon a long life of error and failure." But Blackwell went on to live a remarkably accomplished life. Both she and her sister Elizabeth became physicians. They established one of the first medical schools for other women doctors, the Women's Medical College of the New York Infirmary for Women and Children. Emily Howland, who loved the independence and sense of accomplishment in being away at boarding school, drifted for years after graduation without any sense of purpose. She continued to live with her parents until she was 31, occupying her time with household tasks and family responsibilities. Finally, in 1859, she found her "object in life"—a position as assistant teacher in a school for young black women in Washington, D.C. She devoted the rest of her life to educating and assisting African Americans.

Although they drifted through years of despair and uncertainty, Willard, Howland, and Blackwell, and other women eventually found the work that gave meaning and purpose to their lives. Each had received an education that had prepared and propelled her out into the world. Just as the women's rights movement had begun to raise women's expectations for greater social and political equality, expanding educational opportunities also raised women's aspirations for interesting and useful work—although opportunities to do such work were slow in coming.

By the early 19th century, parents were willing to send daughters as well as sons to school. The two most well-known female academies—Troy Female Seminary and Mount Holyoke Female Seminary—were founded in 1821 and 1837, by Emma Willard and Mary Lyon, respectively. Willard and Lyon were leaders in female education and both wanted to prepare their students to become teachers as well as homemakers. Troy, the first private secondary school for American women, offered a curriculum that included math, science, and teacher-training programs. Many graduates went on to found or teach at other female academies, instilling in their students a profound love of learning and academic excellence.

Mount Holyoke, the first women's college in the United States, also offered a rigorous curriculum. Its three-year course of study

Mount Holyoke Female Seminary in South Hadley, Massachusetts. Its founder, Mary Lyon, wanted to prepare her students to become teachers as well as homemakers.

included English, geography, ancient and modern history, biology, chemistry, mathematics, philosophy, geology, religion, music, French, and gymnastics.

By the 1850s, more academies—such as Mary Sharp College in Winchester, Tennessee; Oxford Female College in Cincinnati, Ohio; and Elmira College in Elmira, New York—had sprung up to educate women. In addition, in 1855, the University of Iowa began to admit both women and men. Antioch College, a private college founded in Yellow Springs, Ohio, in 1852, was also coeducational. Slowly, American women were dismantling the barriers that had prevented them from getting an advanced education. Most of the nation's elite private colleges, such as Harvard, Yale, Princeton, and Amherst, would remain closed to women well into the 20th century. But in the antebellum years, a growing number of institutions were opening their doors to women.

African-American women had fewer educational choices because most public schools and colleges did not accept black students. A few northern cities, such as Boston, established a separate public school for black pupils. Elsewhere, students went to private schools established by black residents or white benefactors. In New Jersey, Sarah Grimké and her sister and brother-in-law, Angelina and Theodore Weld, established an integrated boarding school for both black and white students. The school in Washington, D.C., where Emily Howland taught was the first school to educate black students in that city, which was home to more than 10,000 free blacks.

Mary Jane Patterson graduated from Oberlin in 1862, becoming the first African-American woman to receive a B.A. She became principal of a black high school in Washington, D.C.

Another institution that welcomed African-American students of both sexes was Oberlin College. For black female students in particular, Oberlin offered opportunities unmatched by any other college of the time. Founded in 1833 as a coed institution, Oberlin was the first college to actively recruit both black men and women students. From 1835 to 1865, at least 140 black women attended Oberlin. Most of these students—among them, former slaves—took one or two classes in basic skills, such as reading and writing. Twelve women completed a special "ladies' course," a curriculum that was not as rigorous as the course of study required for a bachelor's degree, and three received their B.A. degrees.

Although Oberlin's black female students usually came from relatively affluent families, some black students at Oberlin had known their share of hardship, including impoverishment or slavery. Frances Jackson, for example, was born into slavery but was freed when her aunt purchased her freedom for $125. The older woman, a former slave herself, had carefully saved the amount out of her own meager wages of $6 a month. After being freed, young Frances Jackson worked as a servant for a wealthy New England family, where she was allowed to study for one hour every other afternoon. In this way, she prepared herself to attend Oberlin. Her aunt provided her tuition.

Fanny Jackson Coppin, a former slave, studied at Oberlin and went on to pursue a distinguished career as an educator. She said later that her goal was "to get an education and become a teacher to my people."

Jackson's course work was demanding: She studied Latin, Greek, and higher math; took private French lessons; and studied piano and guitar. In addition, she taught evening classes to newly freed slaves who were attending a special program at Oberlin, and she was the first black student to teach a preparatory class of both black and white students. Jackson felt tremendous pressure to succeed—as if she had, in her words, "the honor of the whole African race upon my shoulders. I felt that should I fail, it would be ascribed to the fact that I was colored." After graduating, she moved to Philadelphia, where she taught in a black school. Eventually, she became the principal. She was a dedicated educator who inspired her students to become doctors, lawyers, engineers, and teachers.

How did other American women use their educations in the years before the Civil War? They had few choices. Like Jackson, they became teachers because teaching was the principal employment for educated women. Unlike a legal or business career, it did not challenge traditional ideas about women's maternal qualities. Teachers, like mothers, were responsible for educating and instilling a moral code in children. Teaching was regarded as an extension of the mother's role into the classroom.

In the 1830s and 1840s, more teaching opportunities opened up for women because more states required pupils to attend classes for longer terms. During this period, wages for women teachers rose to between $1.50 and $2.00 a week plus board. But women teachers continued to be paid about one-third less than men teachers—another reason why school boards chose to hire more female teachers.

Like Emma Willard and Mary Lyon, Catharine Beecher felt that women were uniquely suited to become teachers because of their superior maternal and moral instincts. She wanted teaching to become a "profession for woman, a profession as honorable and as

Teachers in New Bern, North Carolina, in the 1860s. One teacher of the period wrote, "I know of no more suitable situation for an elderly maiden like myself. I have a nice room neatly furnished, which I occupy alone with my books, the best company I could ask for."

lucrative for her as the legal, medical and theological professions are for men." But instead of establishing one single institution to train women as teachers, she trained and dispatched teachers to open schools throughout the country. She was especially successful in raising money to establish schools in frontier communities. During the 1850s, some 450 teachers trained by her methods opened schools in these towns.

In 1852, Beecher also established the American Woman's Educational Association to finance a women's college that she had established in Milwaukee, Wisconsin. She wanted this college to be the centerpiece of a nationwide system of schools to train women for their "true profession" as educators and homemakers. Although Beecher did not achieve her goal of establishing such a network of schools, she made an immeasurable contribution to opening up more teaching opportunities for women.

As more free black women acquired an education, they became teachers within their own communities. For them, teaching was both a livelihood and a way to help their enslaved brethren. Matilda A. Jones, a star pupil in the only school for blacks in Washington, D.C., explained to a white correspondent, "We need [education] more than your people do, & ought to strive harder, because the greater part of our people, are yet in bondage. We that are free, are expected to be the means of bringing them out of Slavery, & how can we do it, unless we have proper educational advantages? We must get the knowledge, & use it well." During and after the Civil War, scores of dedicated northern black women went South to teach the newly emancipated slaves.

Catharine Beecher believed that women had a high capacity for self-sacrifice, and she took advantage of this virtue in training women as teachers.

Besides teaching, nursing gradually emerged as another occupation for more educated women. Female relatives generally bore responsibility for nursing sick family members, but in the years before the Civil War families occasionally hired nurses. Not until after the Civil War, however, were professional nursing schools established. Until then, nurses learned from experience. Nursing was demanding work. Like a servant, the nurse was on call 24 hours a day. She was not as lowly in status as a servant, nor did she enjoy the prestige of a cook.

But like a servant or a cook, a nurse required great reserves of patience and energy. She spent long hours watching over her patient, preparing special foods and tonics, changing dressings and applying plasters and poultices, and giving massages. A nurse also had to cope with intrusive family members and learn how to bear her patient's suffering and perhaps a lingering death. This was not a job for the timid or weak-hearted, and most paid nurses were older white women who had had years of experience and did not shrink from the sight of a patient's naked body, male or female. Sometimes, the nurse commanded as much authority and respect as a physician, especially when no doctor was available. Nurses earned about three or four dollars a week plus room and board. Employers occasionally added small tips to these wages.

Women who wanted to be doctors instead of nurses faced greater opposition. Until the early part of the 19th century, midwives—women with some medical knowledge—performed deliveries and other medical procedures. Medical practices were based on tradition and folklore,

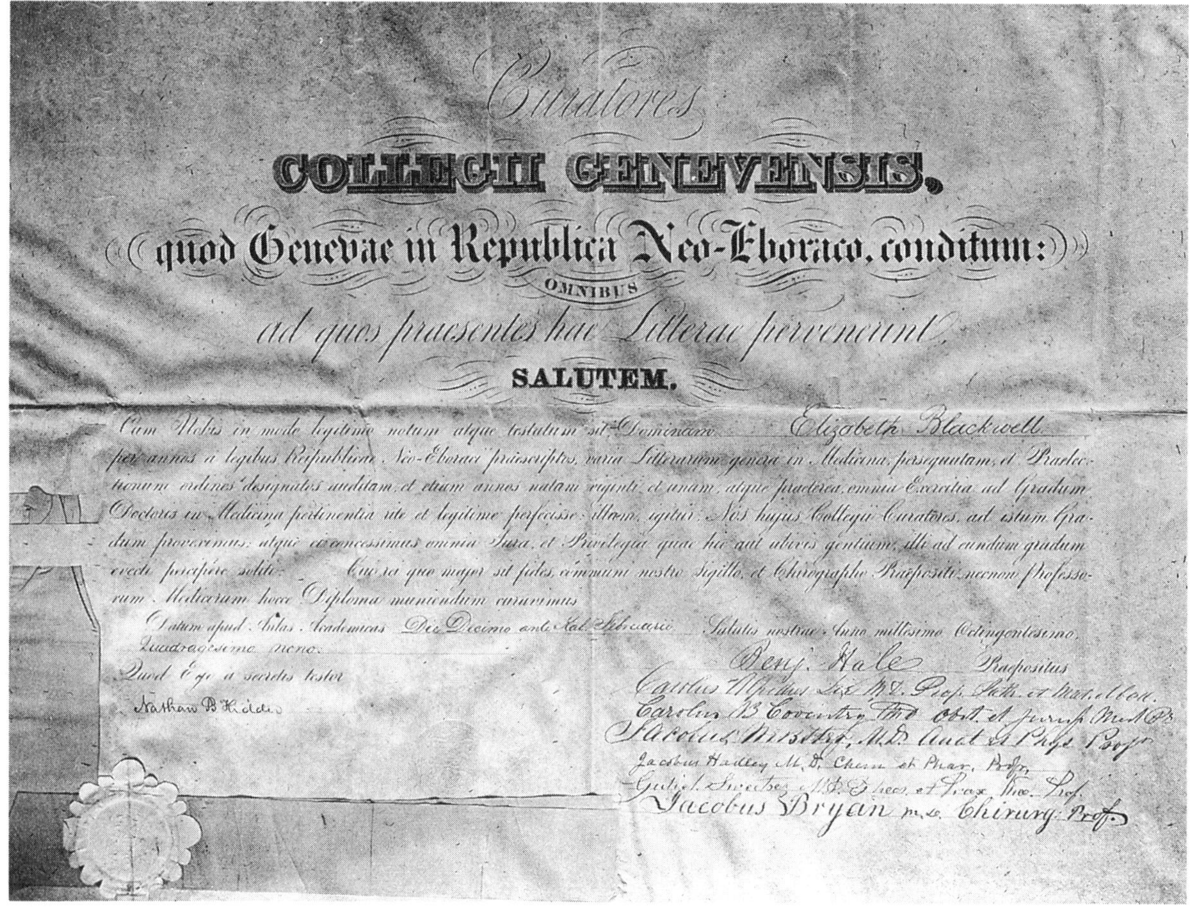

Curatores
COLLEGII GENEVENSIS,
quod Genevae in Republica Neo-Eboraco, conditum:
OMNIBUS
ad quos praesentes hae Litterae pervenerint
SALUTEM.

Cum Nobis in modo legitimo notum atque testatum sit Dominam Elizabeth Blackwell per annos a legibus Reipublicae Neo-Eboraci praescriptos, varia Litterarum genera in Medicina, persequutam, et Praelectionum ordines designatos auditam, et etiam annos natam viginti et unam, atque praeterea omnia Exercitia ad Gradum Doctoris in Medicina pertinentia rite et legitime perfecisse: illam, igitur, Nos hujus Collegii Curatores, ad istum Gradum provenimus, atque ei concessimus omnia Jura et Privilegia quae hic aut ubivis gentium, illi ad eundem gradum evecti percipere soliti. Cujus rei quo major sit fides, communi nostro sigillo, et Chirographo Praepositi, necnon Professorum Medicorum hocce Diploma muniendum curavimus.

Datum apud Aulas Academicas Die Decimo ante Kal. Februarii Salutis nostrae Anno millesimo Octingentesimo Quadragesimo nono.

Quod Ego a secretis testor
Nathan B. Kidder

Benj. Hale Praepositus
Carolus Alfredus Lee M.D. Prof. Path. et Mat. Med.
Carolus B. Coventry M.D. Obst. et Jurisp. Med. Prof.
Jacobus Webster, M.D. Anat. et Phys. Prof.
Jacobus Hadley M.D. Chem. et Phar. Prof.
Gulielmus Sweetser M.D. Theor. et Prax. Med. Prof.
Jacobus Bryan M.D. Chirurg. Prof.

Elizabeth Blackwell received this diploma from Geneva Medical College in 1849, after 27 weeks of study. The Baltimore Sun *lauded her achievement but suggested that she "confine her practice ... to diseases of the heart."*

or on what seemed to work best. The practice of medicine was a craft or an art as much as a science. By the 1830s, however, male physicians attempted to turn medical practice into a profession by requiring special training in accredited schools and special licensing procedures.

These new standards did not necessarily improve the practice of medicine. Even the most educated doctors in these years knew nothing about antibiotics—drugs that kill bacteria and other microorganisms that cause disease—and had only a basic understanding of how the body worked. They used dangerous and painful procedures, such as "bleeding"—the application of leeches to suck out diseased blood from the patient's system—and relied on heavy dosages of laudanum, an addictive drug, to treat pain.

But they succeeded in excluding midwives from medical practice. Medicine was rapidly becoming a profession dominated by men because the new medical schools would not accept women students. In 1847, Elizabeth Blackwell managed to get into Geneva Medical College in upstate New York, despite the faculty's disapproval, because her fellow students, all men, fought for her admission. But when she walked into her first class, as an eyewitness later recalled, a "hush fell upon the class as if each member had been stricken with paralysis." A few years later, Geneva refused to admit any more women.

By the 1850s, enough women, and perhaps some men, believed that women doctors must be trained to treat female patients. Victorian values, which emphasized modesty and little physical or emotional intimacy between men and women, gave further strength to this idea. Male doctors shied away from discussing intimate physiological details with female patients. Indeed, male physicians often conducted examinations of female patients with eyes averted or while the woman was fully clothed—hardly the most effective way to uncover health problems. Although Victorian values defined women's primary role as that of wife and mother, Victorian social practices also paved the way for female doctors who could treat female patients with far greater ease than male doctors could.

Women helped other women receive a medical education. Ann Preston, a Quaker activist in Pennsylvania, solicited funds from more affluent women for a women's medical college in Philadelphia. The school that they endowed, the Female Medical College of Pennsylvania, opened in 1850 and was the first American medical school for women in the United States. Ten years later, the Philadelphia County Medical Society still refused to grant accreditation to the school. In 1855, Preston sent Emmeline Cleveland to France to study obstetrics at a maternity hospital in Paris. Two wealthy women paid for Cleveland's education because they wanted to improve the practice of obstetrics at the Female Medical College. When Cleveland returned, she became head of the school's obstetrics department and one of America's first female physicians.

Other women's medical colleges were also established. In 1856, the New England Female Medical College opened, followed by the Homeopathic New York Medical College for Women in 1863. After the Civil War, more all-male medical schools grudgingly opened their doors to women students.

Law, the other male-dominated profession, adamantly refused to accept women lawyers until the late 1860s and 1870s. Before the Civil War, the primary way to become a lawyer was by studying law independently and then passing the state bar exam, whereupon the candidate was admitted to the bar. Male law students also received practical experience by working as clerks in law offices. Women who had educated themselves in the law were not allowed to take the exam and apply for admission to their state bar. Even Virginia Perry, a strong advocate of opening up more professional opportunities for women, cautioned women against pursuing a legal career because it was not fitting. "The noisy scenes witnessed in a courtroom," she wrote in 1861, "are scarcely compatible with the reserve, quietude and gentleness that characterize a woman of refinement." After the war, however, American women began to challenge the exclusionary practices of their state bars.

Refined women could be writers, and many women earned a living from their writing. Perhaps the most successful novelist of the day was Harriet Beecher Stowe. Sister of Catharine Beecher, Stowe was so moved by a true account of the dramatic escape of a young slave woman and her infant that she sat down and wrote a novel about the evils of southern slavery. She drew on her own observations of slavery while visiting Kentucky and on her years of helping runaway slaves. The result, *Uncle Tom's Cabin,* ran in serial form in an antislavery newspaper for nine months before being published as a book in the spring of 1852. Readers shuddered as they read about the young Eliza's escape across treacherous ice floes and the cruelties visited upon the gentle Tom by his loathsome master, Simon Legree.

Harriet Beecher Stowe, in a daguerreotype made in 1860. She fervently supported the Civil War. "Better a generation should die on the battlefield," she wrote, "that their children may grow up in liberty and justice."

Stowe wished to arouse the nation's conscience to the sin of slavery, and she succeeded spectacularly. The novel was an instant success. Within a year, it had sold 300,000 copies in the United States. Northerners snatched up the novel as proof of the immorality of slavery, while Southerners lambasted Stowe as a "vile wretch in petticoats" for writing such "falsehoods" and "distortions." The novel drew equal attention in Britain and was translated into several foreign languages. When President Abraham Lincoln met Stowe in 1862, he reportedly told her, "So you're the little woman who wrote the book that made this great war." Lincoln was only joking,

This illustration of "Eliza Crossing the Ice" appeared in a French edition of Uncle Tom's Cabin. *The powerful book was translated into several dozen languages.*

but he, like others, recognized the novel's powerful impact upon people's awareness of slavery.

Other women, African-American as well as white, devoted themselves to writing or lecturing about the evils of slavery. Some earned a modest income from their antislavery work. Mary Ann Shadd, the daughter of free blacks who were active in the abolitionist movement, moved for a time to Canada, where she established and edited the *Provincial Freeman* from 1854 to 1859. Shadd believed that blacks would find better employment opportunities and less prejudice in Canada, and she used her journal to urge America's free blacks to migrate to Canada. She also traveled extensively in Canada and the midwestern United States to lecture and raise money for her newspaper. After the war, she helped convert black women to the cause of women's rights.

Frances Ellen Watkins was one of the most effective African-American female lecturers for abolition. Watkins, a poet and former teacher, went on tour for the Maine Antislavery Society. Everywhere

The Webb family toured the country giving public readings from Uncle Tom's Cabin. *Mary Webb (center) also gave readings in England, where the book was a best-seller.*

she spoke, audiences were mesmerized by her strong voice and eloquent words. She used vivid images and uncompromising language. "A hundred thousand new-born babies are annually added to the victims of slavery," she told an audience in 1857. "Twenty thousand lives are annually sacrificed on the plantations of the South. Such a sight should send a thrill of horror through the nerves of civilization and impel the heart of humanity to lofty deeds."

Like their white sisters on the antislavery circuit, Shadd and Watkins braved hazardous winter weather and hostile crowds to bring their message of freedom. But they also suffered from one other hardship—racial prejudice. Watkins described the ordeal of traveling: "On the Carlisle road [in Pennsylvania] I was interrupted and insulted several times. Two men came after me in one day . . . the shadow of slavery, oh, how drearily it hangs."

Other women wrote novels, but their books had none of the fire or drama of *Uncle Tom's Cabin*. Writers such as Fanny Fern, Mrs. E. D. E. N. Southworth, Caroline Kirkland, Catherine Sedgwick, and Caroline Lee Hentz portrayed the peaceful haven of middle-class family life—a home in which a gentle, pure, and morally superior wife and mother reigned supreme and triumphed over the dangerous ideas of male scholars and artists. With their pat characters and plots, these sentimental stories hardly qualified as great literature. But concealed within the sugary prose were some acerbic and astute observations about the powerlessness and sense of entrapment that women felt at home, especially women who had borne large families. Although their books sold well, the contemporary press and some male writers scorned these women. The novelist Nathaniel Hawthorne dismissed them merely as "scribbling women."

As an antislavery lecturer, Frances Ellen Watkins moved audiences to tears with her eloquent descriptions of the horrors of slavery. A gifted poet as well, she taught newly freed slaves during the Civil War and published several volumes of poetry throughout her life.

Women artists also took their themes from the domestic setting of the home. In the 1850s, Lilly Martin Spencer (1822–1902), a self-taught artist, shifted her subject matter from still lifes and themes drawn from mythology and religion to the dailiness of the homemaker's life—cooking, doing laundry, playing with her children. In one painting, a woman wipes her eyes as she peels onions, and in another a housewife extends a flour-covered hand in greeting.

Women painters chose subjects that appealed to their artistic sensibilities and also to popular taste. Although a few women achieved modest success, most female artists lacked the opportunities available to male artists, such as the freedom and means to travel to Europe for study and inspiration. Nor were they allowed to attend classes on figure drawing, where nude male models posed before the class.

But Harriet Hosmer (1830–1908), sculptor and daughter of a physician, managed to take private lessons in anatomy and also traveled to Rome, Italy, for further study. Working each day from dawn to nightfall, Hosmer dedicated her life to her art. She shocked male critics by displaying casts of female nudes in her studio. Complained one critic: "As for Miss Hosmer, her want of modesty is enough to disgust a dog." Male sculptors did not endure such criticism; in-

In her Rome studio, sculptor Harriet Hosmer works on the plaster model of her statue of Thomas Hart Benton. The finished bronze was installed in Lafayette Park in St. Louis, Missouri.

stead, they were expected to draw inspiration from the human body, clothed or unclothed.

Although young women received instruction in painting and needlework at school, few were encouraged to pursue their talent in a career, especially if they married. Jane Swisshelm, a journalist, later bemoaned how she sacrificed her artistic powers to her marriage. "I put away my brushes; resolutely crucified my divine gift, and while it hung writhing on the cross, spent my best years and powers cooking cabbage."

Like Swisshelm, other educated and talented women put away their brushes or their pens to cook cabbages and change diapers. Woman's place, proclaimed the social and religious mores of the day, was in the home as wife and mother. But some women learned to extend the boundaries of women's role to provide more opportunities for women to earn a living.

In years to come, women would take up the banner of motherhood to expand their social roles and political power. The same conception of women's domestic sphere, which had the power to keep women confined to the home as mother and wife, also had the power to expand women's role in American life.

TIME TABLE OF THE LOWELL MILLS,

Arranged to make the working time throughout the year average 11 hours per day.

TO TAKE EFFECT SEPTEMBER 21st., 1853.

The Standard time being that of the meridian of Lowell, as shown by the Regulator Clock of AMOS SANBORN, Post Office Corner, Central Street.

From March 20th to September 19th, inclusive.

COMMENCE WORK, at 6.30 A. M. LEAVE OFF WORK, at 6.30 P. M., except on Saturday Evenings.
BREAKFAST at 6 A. M. DINNER, at 12 M. Commence Work, after dinner, 12.45 P. M.

From September 20th to March 19th, inclusive.

COMMENCE WORK at 7.00 A. M. LEAVE OFF WORK, at 7.00 P. M., except on Saturday Evenings.
BREAKFAST at 6.30 A. M. DINNER, at 12.30 P.M. Commence Work, after dinner, 1.15 P. M.

BELLS.

From March 20th to September 19th, inclusive.

Morning Bells.	*Dinner Bells.*	*Evening Bells.*
First bell,...........4.30 A. M.	Ring out,..............12.00 M.	Ring out,............6.30 P. M.
Second, 5.30 A. M.; Third, 6.20.	Ring in,............12.35 P. M.	Except on Saturday Evenings.

From September 20th to March 19th, inclusive.

Morning Bells.	*Dinner Bells.*	*Evening Bells.*
First bell,...........5.00 A. M.	Ring out,..........12.30 P. M.	Ring out at...........7.00 P. M.
Second, 6.00 A. M.; Third, 6.50.	Ring in,.............1.05 P. M.	Except on Saturday Evenings.

SATURDAY EVENING BELLS.

During APRIL, MAY, JUNE, JULY, and AUGUST, Ring Out, at 6.00 P. M.
The remaining Saturday Evenings in the year, ring out as follows:

SEPTEMBER.

First Saturday, ring out	6.00 P. M.		
Second	"	"	5.45 "
Third	"	"	5.30 "
Fourth	"	"	5.20 "

OCTOBER.

First Saturday, ring out	5.05 P. M.		
Second	"	"	4.55 "
Third	"	"	4.45 "
Fourth	"	"	4.35 "
Fifth	"	"	4.25 "

NOVEMBER.

First Saturday, ring out	4.15 P. M.		
Second	"	"	4.05 "

NOVEMBER.

Third Saturday ring out	4.00 P. M.		
Fourth	"	"	3.55 "

DECEMBER.

First Saturday, ring out	3.50 P. M.		
Second	"	"	3.55 "
Third	"	"	3.55 "
Fourth	"	"	4.00 "
Fifth	"	"	4.00 "

JANUARY.

First Saturday, ring out	4.10 P. M.		
Second	"	"	4.15 "

JANUARY.

Third Saturday, ring out	4.25 P. M.		
Fourth	"	"	4.35 "

FEBRUARY.

First Saturday, ring out	4.45 P. M.		
Second	"	"	4.55 "
Third	"	"	5.00 "
Fourth	"	"	5.10 "

MARCH.

First Saturday, ring out	5.25 P. M.		
Second	"	"	5.30 "
Third	"	"	5.35 "
Fourth	"	"	5.45 "

YARD GATES will be opened at the first stroke of the bells for entering or leaving the Mills.

*** *SPEED GATES commence hoisting three minutes before commencing work.*

CHAPTER 6

Clock of AMOS SAN
From March 20
WORK, at 6.30 A. M.
FAST at 6 A. M. DIN
From Septembe
WORK at 7.00 A. M.
ST at 6.30 A. M. DIN

"I NEVER WORKED SO HARD": WEAVERS, STITCHERS, AND DOMESTICS

While some women cooked cabbages at home, others wove cloth, sewed shoes and shirtwaists, or made umbrellas in noisy, dust-filled factories. Unlike women with more education or money, most working-class women did not have the luxury to think about what kind of work they wanted to do. The skills they possessed, the type of work available to them, and their immediate need for money all determined their choice of work. Many women, and men, had to travel far from their homes in search of work.

As the mighty engines of industry churned and roared, both men and women factory workers felt the impact of dramatic changes in the workplace. In every industry in which they worked, women workers shared three problems—low pay, long hours, and changes in the standards and methods of work. Throughout the antebellum period, factories replaced the home as the place where textiles, shoes, hats, clothing, soap, candles, and other goods were produced.

Although women had always worked for long hours, the factory system imposed new hardships. Most striking, women had no control over the rates they charged for their work or the hours they worked; they received a wage determined by a boss, and they were expected to work fixed hours.

The Lowell Mills in Massachusetts ran on a strict schedule that was signaled by the ringing of bells. The women worked a 12-hour day with 45 minutes off for lunch.

To make matters worse, opportunities for wage work both at home and in the factory diminished because more women were

Tenements in New York City were overcrowded and unsanitary and became breeding grounds for such deadly diseases as tuberculosis. Many tenement dwellers did piecework at home and had little chance to escape their dismal surroundings.

vying for work. Part of the competition came from immigrant women, especially the growing influx of Irish. By the 1850s, Irish immigrants replaced native-born women in the textile factories of New England. In addition, when women tried new kinds of wage labor, such as office work, they faced strong opposition from male employees.

These were not easy years for women workers, nor for men workers. Single wage earners as well as entire families were barely making ends meet on meager wages, and thousands of Americans lived in damp, overcrowded, and unventilated cellar rooms. In Boston, the Committee on Internal Health reported that in slum districts, residents were "huddled together like brutes without regard to sex, age or a sense of decency, grown men and women sleeping together in the same apartment, and sometimes wife, husband, brothers and sisters in the same bed."

In 1851, Horace Greeley, editor of the *New York Tribune,* estimated that $10.37 was the minimum weekly wage necessary to support a family of five. This would pay for rent, food, fuel, and clothing. But, Greeley observed, this income allowed for no luxuries and no money left to pay medical bills.

Yet, in 1851, most urban workers hardly made $10.37 a week. A shoemaker or printer averaged $4 to $6, and a cabinetmaker made about $5 a week. Male textile workers made $6.50; female textile workers averaged about $3.50. To make ends meet, entire families—children as well as adults—went to work in factories or did piecework at home. They often worked 12 to 16 hours a day, and earned a dollar a day between them.

Single factory women were especially hard-pressed. Although their wages did not rise, their cost of living did. In 1845, according to the *New York Tribune,* the average female factory hand made $2 a week, but room and board cost about $1.50 to $1.75 a week, leaving only 50 cents for clothing, medicine, church dues, leisure activities, and savings. Even a brief period of unemployment could be disastrous because it could use up all of a worker's savings. By 1861, average wages had not risen, but the cost of room and board in urban areas had increased to about $2, the same as a wage earner's weekly income. Women workers now had no money left for other expenses.

In almost every industry, women usually earned only half to

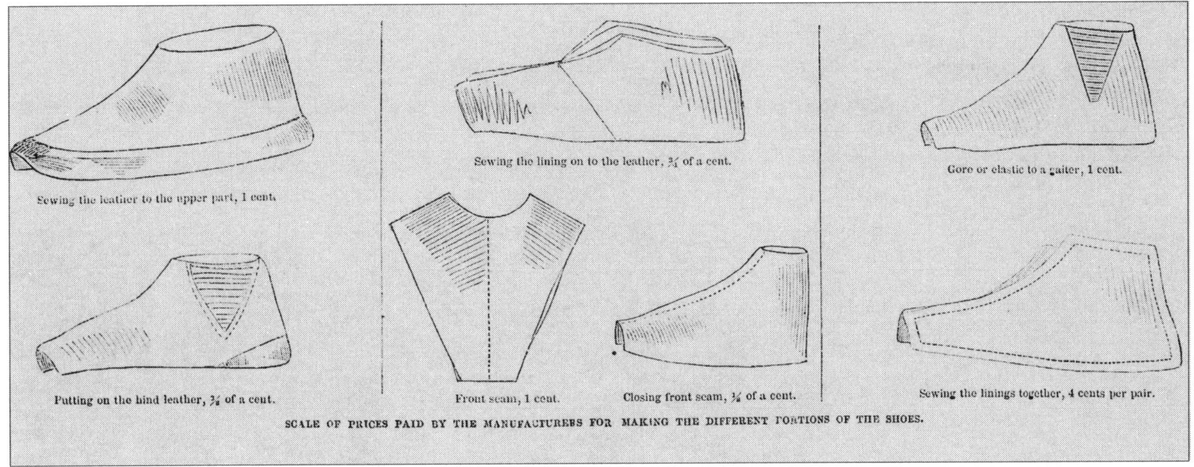

This diagram shows the prices paid by Massachusetts shoe manufacturers for the various parts of a shoe. Workers were paid by the piece.

two-thirds of what men earned. Even the most highly skilled women often did not earn as much as the lowest-paid man. Employers justified paying lower wages to women because they, and most of American society, viewed them as temporary workers whose true place was in the home.

This narrow view of women's lives prevented people from improving working conditions for female wage workers or insisting that more occupations open up for women workers. Just as women were not suited to the noisy scenes of the courtroom as lawyers, people argued, neither were their "delicate" natures suited to the hurly-burly of the factory floor. And, indeed, most women stopped doing regular wage work once they married. Only the poorest married women continued to work outside of the home.

The impact of both new technology and the growing influx of immigrant workers can best be seen in the New England textile mills. In the 1820s and 1830s, young women from the farm country of New England went to work in the massive brick textile factories springing up along the Merrimack River near Lowell, Massachusetts, and other New England towns. In 1820, Lowell—then called East Chelmsford—was a sleepy village of about 200 farm families, located about 25 miles northwest of Boston. Six years later, it had grown into a town of 2,500 and was incorporated as the town of Lowell. In 1830, the population surged to 6,000, and tripled to 18,000 just six years later. By 1850, Lowell boasted a population of 33,000. What created this booming growth was the rise of the textile industry. Other New England mill towns also grew, but Lowell quickly

The Middlesex Mills in Lowell, Massachusetts, about 1848. Immigrant workers gradually took over as American-born women left to get married or take higher-paying work in the cities.

became the center of the New England textile industry and drew workers—mostly single women as young as 16 or 17—from across New England.

These women generally came from the middle ranks of farm families, those that were neither impoverished nor wealthy. The desire to be financially and socially independent, to finance an education, or simply to experience the pleasures of living and working in a larger town drew many young farm women to the mills. Some women did contribute their earnings to their families, but mostly they worked in the mills to earn their own income. In 1851, Lucy Ann, a mill worker in Clinton, Massachusetts, wrote to her cousin: "I have earned enough to school me awhile, & have not I a right to do so . . . I merely wish to go to [Oberlin] because I think it the best way of spending the money I have worked so hard to earn."

Although young women had worked long hours doing chores on the family farm, mill work was a far cry from the pace and rate of work at home. Even the mills themselves—massive five- to six-story brick structures that employed 250 to 300 workers each—contrasted starkly to the homey, weather-beaten farmhouses familiar to most young workers. Each floor of the mill was devoted to a different task, such as carding (preparing the cotton fibers for spinning by removing dirt and other impurities), spinning, dressing (preparing the yarn for weaving), and weaving. An elevator connected the different floors to move materials from one step in the production process to another.

The work was repetitive, the machinery loud and cumbersome, and the workrooms filled with the flying dust of cotton fibers. Young women stood or sat at their machines for 12 hours a day, six days a week, breathing in this unhealthy dust. The work was also dangerous. A Polish worker in a Lawrence, Massachusetts, mill caught her hair in her machine. Seconds later, she lay writhing in agony on the floor, part of her scalp torn off. Her co-workers salvaged the piece of scalp and took her to a doctor. Fortunately, she survived.

Until 1847, women worked 12 hours a day, six days a week. That year, they received an extra half-hour for dinner, reducing the work day to about 11 hours. The working day usually started at 5:00 A.M. and ended at 7:00 P.M. Workers had a 35-minute break for breakfast at 7:00 A.M. and a 45-minute dinner break at noon. In 1853, the workday was cut again, to 11 hours, six days a week.

Until the early 1850s, female mill workers were expected to live in the boardinghouses provided by the mill owners. Built of brick, these structures lay across from the mills. Separate tenements housed the families of married workers, who, until the 1850s, were mostly men. Female mill hands shared tiny rooms—usually four to a room—and took all of their meals at the boardinghouse.

Mill owners insisted that their female hands be in their boardinghouses by 10 o'clock each evening, and they urged boarding-

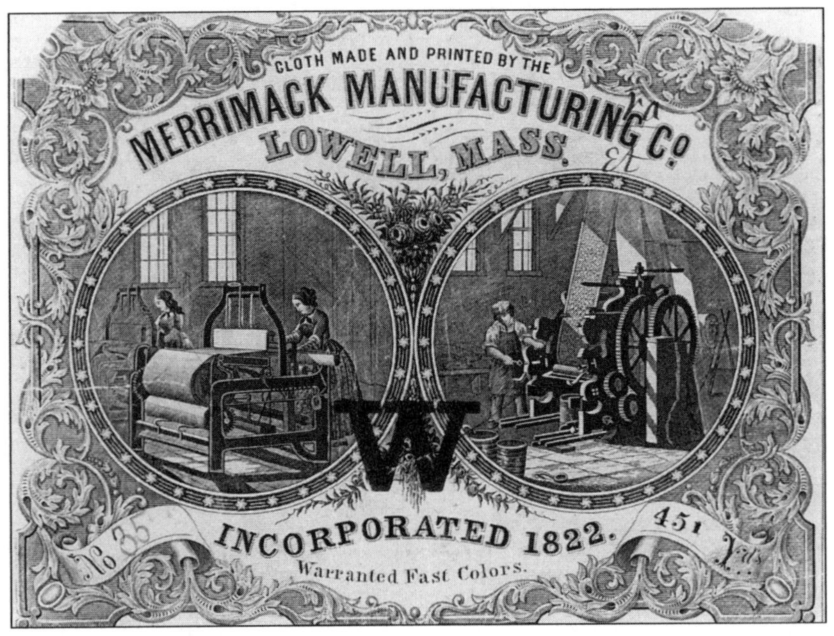

Cloth manufactured by the Merrimack Manufacturing Co. bore this label, which showed female weavers and a male mechanic. Even in plants where both men and women worked as weavers, the women earned about one-third less.

house keepers, usually older women, to report any violators to the management. In the early years, women were required to attend church services regularly, and some mill owners even deducted pew rent from the women's earnings and paid it directly to local churches.

These close living and working arrangements created a camaraderie among the women workers, a community of like-minded women who eagerly wanted to improve their minds and their lives. Throughout the 1830s and 1840s, they organized and attended lectures, language classes, sewing groups, and literary "improvement circles"—after working a 12-hour day. From one of these circles was born the *Lowell Offering,* the first journal ever written by and for mill women. The journal published poetry, short stories, and commentary penned by the female workers.

Workers also organized themselves into labor-reform groups to crusade for better working conditions and shorter workdays. As technological innovations enabled women to work faster and produce more, mill owners assigned more machines to workers—without raising wages. For example, at Hamilton Company, one of the mills in Lowell, the average number of looms per weaver more than doubled between 1840 and 1854. The workload for spinners increased as well. Workers were expected to operate more machines at a faster rate. But wages remained the same—although the company reaped higher profits from the workers' increased productivity. Indeed, in the fall of 1848, wages were reduced in all of the Lowell mills, but the workload

Mill work was tedious as well as dangerous. Workers hoisted heavy equipment, worked long hours, breathing in the cotton dust, and risked getting their fingers and hair caught in the equipment.

REGULATIONS

To be observed by all Persons employed by the Proprietors of the Tremont Mills.

THE Overseers are to be punctually in their Rooms at the starting of the Mill, and not to be absent unnecessarily during working hours. They are to see that all those employed in their rooms are in their places in due season, and keep a correct account of their time and work. They may grant leave of absence to those employed under them when there are spare hands in the room to supply their places; otherwise they are not to grant leave of absence except in cases of absolute necessity.

All persons in the employ of the Proprietors of the Tremont Mills, are required to observe the regulations of the room where they are employed. They are not to be absent from their work without consent, except in case of sickness, and then they are to send the Overseer word of the cause of their absence.

They are to board in one of the Boarding houses belonging to the Company, and conform to the regulations of the house where they board.

The Company will not employ any one who is habitually absent from public worship on the Sabbath.

All persons entering into the employment of the Company are considered as engaging to work twelve months.

All persons intending to leave the employment of the Company are to give two week's notice of their intention to their Overseer; and their engagement with the Company is not considered as fulfilled, unless they comply with this regulation.

Payments will be made monthly, including board and wages, which will be made up to the last Saturday of every month, and paid in the course of the following week.

These Regulations are considered a part of the contract with all persons entering into the employment of the Proprietors of the TREMONT MILLS.

J. AIKEN, AGENT.

The Tremont Mills had strict rules for their workers, who were required to live in company housing and to attend church regularly.

was as demanding as ever. On November 5, 1848, Mary Paul, from Vermont, wearily wrote her father, "I never worked so hard in my life but perhaps I shall get used to it."

Throughout the 1840s, every year brought new pressures on mill workers to work harder, faster, and longer. And every year, starting in 1842, workers circulated petitions for a 10-hour day. Some female workers, however, were reluctant to complain because they planned to work only a few more years before marrying and did not want to jeopardize their opportunity to make as much money as they could.

By 1848, native-born farm women no longer flocked to the mills at Lowell or elsewhere. The notorious workload, made worse by

The Lowell Offering *published the writing of "factory girls." After working 12 hours a day, these inspired young women wrote poetry, fiction, book reviews, and articles in support of women's rights. Bravely, they also urged reforms in the workplace, such as a shorter workday and higher wages.*

assigning more and faster machines to each worker, and the opportunity to secure other work, such as teaching, drew women away from the mills. In their place came immigrant men and women. By 1852, half of all factory operatives in the New England mills were foreign born. Most of these new mill workers were Irish, and they snatched the lowest-paying and least-skilled jobs, such as carding and spinning, while native-born women monopolized the more skilled jobs. Irish workers also lived separately from native-born women, who refused to live or work with them. Gradually, Irish operatives moved into higher-paying positions.

Like other working-class families in the 1850s, immigrant families made mill work a family affair. From the ages of 6 to 9, immigrant mill workers' children attended school. But by 13, girls began to work in the mills. Boys, by contrast, started working around age 15. Families wanted their daughters to work as long as possible before they left the work force to marry. Unlike American-born workers, who generally kept all of their earnings, an immigrant daughter turned over a large part of her earnings to her family out of economic necessity as well as a strong sense of family obligation.

New technology also altered women's work in other industries. As more women sought work as seamstresses, sewing women's wages declined. In 1845, the *New York Daily Tribune* estimated that twice as many women were seeking work as seamstresses "as would find employment at fair wages." On the average, dressmakers who worked in factories 16 hours a day made $1.25 to $2.50 a week in the 1850s. Those who worked at home, sewing bundles of cloth picked up from contractors—middlemen who represented garment manufacturers—made even less. Capmakers, who worked 15 to 18 hours a day, usually at home, were the lowest paid of all garment workers. Their average wage was 14 cents a day, or about 84 cents a week.

Out of these meager wages, all sewers paid for thread and needles and any damage to the garment, such as tears. In cities such as Boston and New York, where a single woman needed to earn at least three dollars a week, these wages were hardly adequate. Some women turned to prostitution to supplement their wages. How other workers survived is a mystery.

A poem by Edward Zane Carroll, published in 1849, aptly described the seamstress's plight:

A merchant in Milledgeville, Illinois, ran this 1855 ad touting his economical ready-made clothes. Low wages and efficient sewing machines enabled manufacturers to charge competitive prices.

We are many in the city
  Who the weary needle ply;
None to aid and few to pity
  Tho' we sicken down and die;
But tis work, work away
  By night and by day
Oh, tis work, work away
  We've no time to pray.

In 1846, Elias Howe introduced the first sewing machine. Five years later, in 1851, the addition of a foot treadle for easier operation made the machine an indispensable tool. But instead of easing the sewer's burden, the sewing machine increased it.

Hand sewers could no longer compete with the sewing machine. In one day, one sewing machine operator could do as much work as six hand sewers. Hand sewers were forced to buy or rent sewing machines, or work in garment factories, where they had no control over their wages or hours.

To make matters worse, seamstresses, like the mill workers of New England, were expected to work faster and produce more while working for the same wages. New technology, such as the sewing machine or improved looms, enabled consumers to buy manufactured goods at reasonable prices—but at the expense of factory workers, who were not paid a fair wage for operating this new technology.

Some sewers took matters into their own hands. In 1850, women tailors in Philadelphia organized a cooperative to make and sell clothing as well as to hire out their services for mending and tailoring. "We are industrious and willing to work," they declared, "but paid as we are, we can not get enough to support life." Lucretia Mott and others assisted them in organizing. The cooperative lasted at least two years, then lost momentum and disbanded.

In 1851, 6,000 stitchers in New York City followed suit and united to form the Shirt Sewers Cooperative Union. They decided to divide both the work and profits among themselves. Through letters in sympathetic newspapers, they appealed for public support and contributions to help them get started, and the funds came pouring in. The union hired a director, rented a store, and began to fill orders for shirts. According to the *New York Daily Tribune,* the Shirt Sewers Cooperative Union was "among the successful combinative efforts at work in this city." Again, the cooperative seems to have dwindled and disappeared within a few years of its founding.

The mere act of joining a cooperative required great courage. Many parents, religious leaders, newspaper editors, and factory owners disapproved of any challenge to authority, especially from women, who were supposed to cultivate the proper feminine traits of deference and daintiness. Moreover, factory owners and managers did not care about their employees, who worked in ill-ventilated and ill-lit rooms at machines that could ensnare fingers or long hair. Workers were cogs in a machine that was devoted to production and profits. "I regard my work-people just as I regard my machinery," claimed one factory supervisor. "When my machines get old and useless, I

In the late 1850s, Thomson's Shirt Manufactory in New York City employed 1,000 girls who operated 500 machines. They turned out 3,000 to 4,000 dresses daily.

reject them and get new [machines], and these people are part of my machinery."

In other industries, the story was much the same. New technology undercut the independent worker, forcing people to work in new factories or to purchase expensive machinery to use at home. Until 1852, women shoebinders in Massachusetts worked mostly part time at home, sewing the upper part of the shoe by hand. That year, a new Singer sewing machine, able to stitch leather, was introduced in the shoe factories of Massachusetts. Some female shoebinders feared the new machine would displace them. At one demonstration of the new equipment in 1853, according to an eyewitness account, female onlookers "shook their fists" at the agent demonstrating the equipment because he was destroying their livelihood.

Soon, however, women began to work in the factories using these new machines. Although they earned higher wages working full-time in the factory, the fears of those fist-shaking women came true. One woman working full-time at her machine accomplished as much as 11 shoebinders working by hand. Consequently, the number of women employed in shoe manufacturing declined dramatically throughout the 1850s. But the increased productivity of these female machine operators created a greater demand for male workers, who did the skilled work of cutting the leather and making the parts of the shoe. Fewer female operators were hired, but additional male shoemakers were recruited. And though wages almost doubled for female operators throughout the 1850s, women who continued to sew at home by hand received lower wages because they could not maintain the pace or productivity of their factory counterparts.

The shoemakers of Lynn, Massachusetts, went on strike in 1859. They marched through the snow, preceded by the band of the Lynn City Guards, with a banner that read: "American ladies will not be slaves. Give us a fair compensation and we will labour cheerefully."

For a time, however, female shoebinders who sewed by hand at home and those who sewed by machine in the shop joined forces. In 1860, male and female shoe workers in Lynn, Massachusetts, struck for better wages. This was the largest labor protest by American workers before the Civil War. As many as 6,000 workers—5,000 men and 1,000 women—joined the strike, carrying banners proclaiming "American Ladies Will Not Be Slaves."

The female factory shoebinders realized that their work was crucial to the total production process. They urged shoebinders who worked at home to join them in demanding higher wages for all female shoebinders, those who worked at home as well as in the factory. As the strike spread to other shoe-producing towns in eastern Massachusetts, the Lynn shoebinders attempted to recruit shoebinders in these other towns to join them.

Their coalition thrived briefly, but male strikers insisted that wage increases for men were more important because higher wages for them meant they could better support their families. They convinced many women shoebinders that increasing the wages of female factory workers would eliminate the need for women to work at home part-time to supplement their husbands' higher earnings. They harkened back to an earlier time when men were the main breadwinners and women, as subordinates to men, worked only part-time while tending to their families.

Deserted by their fellow shoebinders who worked at home, the factory shoebinders beseeched their former allies to support them once again. But the home workers stood firm, and the factory shoebinders dropped out of the strike. Upholding traditional images of women, the home workers supported the male strikers by carrying banners that proclaimed "weak in physical strength but strong in moral courage, we dare to battle for the right shoulder to shoulder with our fathers, husbands and brothers." With them went a powerful source of labor protest that could have strengthened the grievances of all the workers—male and female—against the unfair labor practices of factory owners.

Despite the long hours and low wages, women still preferred working in factories to being domestic servants. At least factory workers had some free time; servants were on call 24 hours a day. Domestics worked up to 16 hours a day, with one afternoon off each week. They earned $1 to $1.25 a week plus board. Servants' duties varied according to their employers' requirements and the number of other servants employed in the house. But in general, the work was very demanding. Domestics devoted entire days to washing, baking, ironing, and cleaning each room. They were accustomed to heavy physical work—cleaning out fireplaces or emptying chamber pots—and trudging up and down staircases several times a day.

Besides enduring the back-breaking work, servants also had to endure the snobbery of their social "superiors." During the colonial era, servants were treated as part of the family and joined in all household activities. By the mid-19th century, however, they were regarded as mere hired hands, and were viewed as an inferior class. The Boston census of 1845 categorized servants as part of the "unclassified residue of the population." No wonder that young women wanted to avoid the social stigma of being a domestic. Mary Paul, who left the Lowell mills to live and work in an experimental community, observed that many women "would live on 25 cts per week at sewing, or school teaching rather than work at housework. . . . This all comes from the way servants are treated."

At a February 1860 meeting, the women of Lynn debated the proper wages for various jobs. The debate was reported in detail in both Boston and New York newspapers.

But Irish and free black women often had no choice because they could not find work elsewhere. They made up the bulk of women domestics. Some Irish women even preferred domestic work because the free room and board enabled them to save more of their wages

The Pemberton Mill in Lawrence, Massachusetts, collapsed and burned in January 1860, resulting in massive injuries and loss of life. Rescuers worked through the night to recover victims, mostly young women.

and learn about American customs and manners more easily. By 1855, 25 percent of all Irish immigrant women and 50 percent of all free black women worked as servants. Domestic service employed the largest number of all working women. Free black women also worked as washerwomen, seamstresses, and dressmakers. All of these jobs were laborious and low-paying.

When they could not make ends meet on meager salaries, some female wage earners turned to prostitution as a last, desperate resort. In 1859, William Sanger, a social investigator, published a report of his research into the lives of 2,000 female prostitutes serving time in New York's Blackwell's Island prison. He discovered that nearly a fourth of the women had worked in the sewing trades and that almost half of the prostitutes had been servants, making $5 or less a month. Many of the women claimed they were destitute when they turned to prostitution and had no other way to earn enough to support themselves.

As the storm clouds of Civil War gathered over the nation, the final curtain on this difficult era for wage-earning men and women came, fittingly enough, in the form of a tragedy. On January 10, 1860, the Pemberton Mill, a textile mill in Lawrence, Massachusetts, collapsed. Like a structure made out of matchsticks, the mill folded in on itself. About 900 workers were inside—mostly women. Throughout that day and into the night, the townspeople of Lawrence frantically dug through the rubble of brick and twisted, torn machinery to rescue the trapped mill workers.

At 11:00 o'clock that night, a huge fire erupted, but the rescue work continued. Eighty-eight mill workers had died, 116 were severely wounded, and another 159 workers had sustained less serious injuries. An investigation was made and the accident was attributed to faulty construction. The engineer in charge of construction, who had known that the foundation was not strong enough to withstand the weight of the building, was merely censured.

Although mercy was shown to the engineer, little or none was extended to the victims of the tragedy. Workers who survived the collapse were left unemployed, with no savings to support them until they found other work. One female worker told a relief committee that she owed her boarding lady for her room and board, but, according to a relief committee report, the woman was "unwilling to keep her as she is out of work."

American workers did achieve some small victories during the late 1840s and 1850s, however. In Pennsylvania, Massachusetts, New Hampshire, and some other states, workers succeeded in passing state laws providing for 10-hour workdays and longer periods of schooling for children who worked. But their victory was incomplete. With reduced hours came reduced wages, and some employers made workers sign contracts agreeing to work longer days when necessary.

Growing industrialization did provide women with new ways to earn a living—but the living they earned in those noisy, dangerous factories barely supported them. And the relentless factory bell and production quotas harshly reminded them of their lack of power over working conditions and hours. Women left the factories as soon as they could, by marrying or by finding better-paying or more desirable work, such as teaching.

But the vast majority of working women had neither the luxury of an education nor a breadwinner who could support them. By 1860, only about 15 percent of all American women worked for wages, and most of them were among the poorer classes—free black and immigrant women, widows, and rural migrants to the growing cities. But the guns of war would soon change the kind of jobs available to women. From the terrible tragedy of Civil War would come new and different wage-earning opportunities for all women.

"I AM NEEDED HERE": WOMEN AT WAR

Like a fire bell in the night—the fire bell that Thomas Jefferson had feared so many years before—shots pierced the dawn silence in Charleston, South Carolina, on April 12, 1861. Confederate troops had fired on a U.S. garrison at Fort Sumter, in Charleston Harbor. Although no one was killed in the ensuing skirmish, those early-morning shots ignited the bloodiest war in the nation's history.

After 33 hours of constant bombardment, Major Robert Anderson, commander of the U.S. garrison at the fort, surrendered. On April 14, the Stars and Stripes was lowered and the Confederate stars and bars triumphantly raised over Fort Sumter. The Civil War had begun, and both sides—Union and Confederacy—erupted in celebration, as if a giant party had commenced. In Richmond, Virginia, the Confederate capital, everyone "seemed to be perfectly frantic with delight," an observer wrote. "I never in all my life witnessed such excitement." Troops drilled and marched through the city to the fervent cheers of thousands of bystanders. "The town is crowded with soldiers," Mary Boykin Chesnut reported in her diary. "These new ones are running in. . . . They fear the war will be over before they get a sight of the fun."

The news of Sumter's capture electrified Northerners as well, and a wave of patriotic fervor swept through the North. In New York City, a quarter of a million people flocked to a giant rally for the Union. Across the North, people swarmed into the streets wav-

Surrounded by military officers, this woman posed as Miss Liberty in a photograph used for fund-raising for soldiers' relief activities.

After the fall of Fort Sumter in April 1861, crowds rallied in New York's aptly named Union Square to support the Union cause.

ing Union flags. "The people have gone stark mad!" exclaimed a woman in the Midwest.

Both the North and the South were jubilant about going to war. Northerners believed that they were fighting to preserve the country, while Southerners believed that they were putting their lives on the line to preserve not only slavery but a whole way of life. Each side believed that the war would be over in a matter of weeks and that its soldiers would win, resolving once and for all the long years of debate and painful compromise over slavery.

Abraham Lincoln's election to the Presidency was the climax to this agonizing drama over slavery. Southerners portrayed him as a "Black Republican" who would overthrow slavery and give all African Americans as much, if not more, political power than whites. "Do you love your mother, your wife, your sister, your daughter?" a Georgia official demanded of nonslaveholders after Lincoln's election. If Georgia remained in a Union "ruled by Lincoln and his crew . . . in TEN years or less our CHILDREN will be the slaves of negroes."

Events moved rapidly toward disunion after Lincoln's election. On February 9, 1861, Jefferson Davis, a senator and former secretary of war, was elected president of the Confederate States of America. The CSA consisted of South Carolina, Georgia, Florida, Alabama, Mississippi, Louisiana, and Texas. Virginia joined the Confederacy three days after Fort Sumter was captured, and North Carolina, Tennessee, and Arkansas did the same over the next three months. The rest of the slaveholding states—Delaware, Maryland, Kentucky, and Missouri—remained in the Union, but their loyalties lay partly with the Confederacy.

Lincoln opposed slavery, but he had no intention of interfering with it in the states where it already existed. He even believed that the Constitution protected slavery in those states, though he hoped that slavery would eventually die out on its own.

Southern women zealously supported the southern cause of independence. A Georgia woman wrote her local newspaper, "I feel a new life within me, and my ambition aims at nothing higher than to become an ingenious, economical, industrious housekeeper, and an independent Southern woman." Throughout the South, women urged their menfolk to enlist in the Confederate military. A Selma, Alabama, woman even broke off her engagement when her fiancé failed to enlist. She sent him a skirt and pantaloons with a note attached: "Wear these or volunteer."

Up North, women also showed passionate support—for the Union. Shortly after the war began, Louisa May Alcott, who later wrote the novel *Little Women,* confided in her diary, "I long to be a man; but as I can't fight, I will content myself with working for those who can." Harriet Beecher Stowe called the Union effort a "cause to die for," and a woman in New York declared, "It seems as if we never were alive till now; never had a country till now."

As their husbands and sons drilled and marched and prepared for battle in opposing armies, women of the North and South swung

The ladies of the Pennsylvania Academy of Fine Arts sewed enormous flags for the soldiers to carry into battle.

into action. Throughout the North, women organized soldiers' aid societies to sew uniforms, assemble medical supplies, and knit scarves, socks, mittens, and other items for Union soldiers.

In Troy, New York, educator Emma Willard became president of her newly organized society. Her group immediately applied for a government contract to sew soldiers' uniforms and give soldiers' wives paid employment. In New York City, about 60 women met at the New York Infirmary for Women and Children, the hospital founded by physicians Elizabeth and Emily Blackwell, to organize the relief efforts of New York City's women. Within a few days, the Woman's Central Association of Relief (WCAR) was formed with an initial membership of 2,000 to 3,000 women. Befitting a city the size of New York, the WCAR became the largest women's organization to carry out soldiers' relief work.

Unlike earlier volunteer groups, these soldiers' relief societies introduced a new concept to volunteer work: efficiency. During the antebellum years, women who did volunteer work were inspired by religious and moral ideals, and were infused with a moral and spiritual zeal. Now, as the huge task of supplying the food, clothing, and medical needs of northern soldiers got underway, volunteers were inspired by the precepts of business rather than religion. They felt an abiding, even motherly concern for the soldiers' welfare, but discipline and efficiency, cooperation and coordination, became the watchwords on their lips.

Free African-American women of the North also did relief work,

Physician Elizabeth Blackwell organized a meeting of 3,000 women at the Cooper Union in New York City to form the Woman's Central Association of Relief for the Union army. They provided valuable nursing services, among other contributions.

TO THE

Patriotic Women of Philadelphia.

A meeting of the Ladies of the City of Philadelphia will be held this day, at 4 o'clock, P. M., at the School Room, in Tenth Street, one door above Spring Garden St., west side, to devise means to give aid and comfort to our noble Soldiers, who have volunteered for the defence of our outraged Flag.

Contributions will be thankfully accepted of such materials as may be found useful to the Volunteers.

In times like these, when our Husbands, Fathers, Sons and Brothers are doing battle for the honor of our common country, let the women be not behind-hand in bestowing their aid and sympathy.

MANY LADIES.

CONCERT!

FOR THE BENEFIT OF

The Soldiers.

Greensboro Female College.

A Concert will be held in the *College Chapel* on the night of the 20th inst., for the benefit of our volunteers. Doors open at 6 and a half o'clock. Exercises will commence at 7.

☞ Price of admission 50 cents. Children 25.

In both the North and South, women on the home front raised money to support their troops. The poster at left advertised a Philadelphia relief meeting; the one above announced a benefit concert at a women's college in North Carolina.

primarily for former slaves who had escaped North or who were liberated by Union troops as they advanced into Confederate states. In Lawrence, Kansas, for example, the Ladies' Refugee Aid Society helped former slaves find housing in Kansas. Elsewhere, free black women raised money to assist ex-slaves.

Harriet Jacobs, a former slave herself, assisted freedpeople who were flocking to Washington, D.C., in search of shelter and employment. At Freedmen's Village, a temporary community where more than 1,000 former slaves were raising food for the Union army, she distributed clothing to the needy, nursed sick refugees, helped other refugees find work, and organized sewing circles and schools. Jacobs derived great satisfaction from her work. "The good God has spared me for this work," she wrote a correspondent. "The last six months have been the happiest of all my life."

Sojourner Truth, the former slave who mesmerized audiences with her eloquence, also worked as a counselor at Freedmen's Village. There, she instructed former slaves "in the habits of industry and economy," as she wrote a friend. "Many of them are entirely ignorant of housekeeping [but] they all want to learn the way we live in the North," she explained. Truth also taught home economics and personal hygiene to freedwomen. Like Jacobs, she felt truly fulfilled by this work. "I think I am doing good," she wrote. "I am needed here."

In the South, white Confederate women were immersed in soldiers' relief efforts as well. Indeed, in Charleston, South Carolina, women had started rolling bandages in January 1861, three months before the war had even begun. Shortly after the war started, women throughout the Confederacy organized hundreds of local soldiers' relief societies. In South Carolina alone, more than 150 such societies sprang up in the first two months of war. Women in Petersburg, Virginia, met every day, including Sundays, to sew uniforms and knit socks and blankets for Confederate soldiers.

Many of these soldiers' relief groups had once been benevolent reform and missionary societies. Now, they turned from raising money for their churches or charitable activities to outfitting their soldiers. Knitting needles flew like whirligigs and sewing machines whirred nonstop as women dashed off one uniform after another.

But southern women did more than knit socks—they also filled cartridges and made sandbags for fortification. Because the South

Despite severe hardship at home, Southern women urged their beaux to go off to fight for the Confederate cause, and they industriously sewed uniforms for the soldiers. This engraving appeared shortly after the war in a book entitled Picture of the Desolated States.

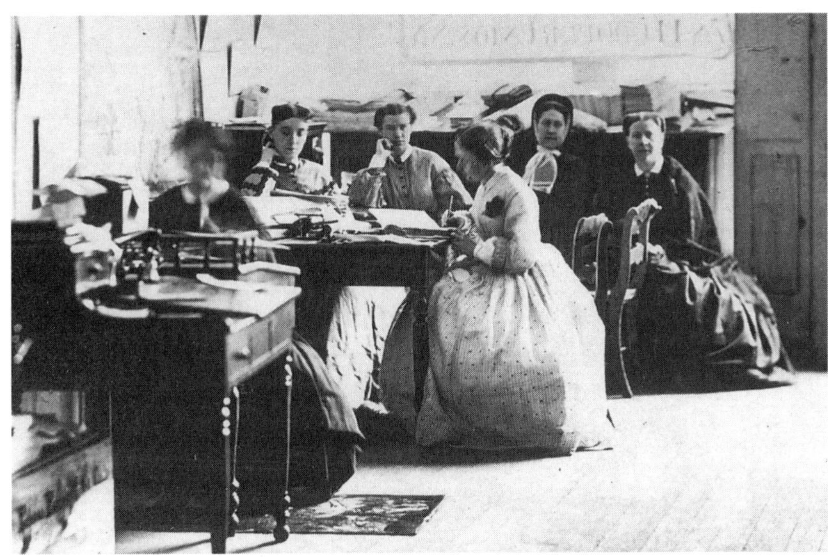

This rare photograph shows the women of the Woman's Central Association of Relief doing paperwork in their New York office.

had fewer factories than the North for making weapons and other war supplies, those back home—mostly women—were pressed into volunteer service to make vital war materiel. Some women were paid for their efforts, especially when they worked in the few factories that did exist, but most women volunteered their services.

Through their soldiers' relief work, both northern and southern women, African-American as well as white, developed valuable administrative skills. They learned how to coordinate the flow of money and supplies from their groups to other agencies or to the soldiers themselves. They also learned how to keep records, act as leaders of their own groups, and make important decisions regarding the way they used their time, energies, and money. Like their sisters in the women's rights movement and in earlier volunteer groups, they were learning how to be leaders and policymakers.

During the war, women's rights activists continued to draft petitions and collect signatures—but on behalf of African-American slaves instead of for themselves. In 1863, Elizabeth Cady Stanton and Susan B. Anthony organized the National Women's Loyal League to work for the abolition of slavery in all states, including slaveholding states that supported the Union. Both abolitionists and women's rights activists joined the league, and its membership quickly rose to 5,000. In less than a year, the league collected almost 400,000 signatures on petitions urging Congress to pass a 13th constitutional amendment abolishing slavery. Like soldiers' relief societies, the league

Under the supervision of an army officer, women at the federal arsenal in Watertown, Massachusetts, fill cartridges with gunpowder. About 100,000 Northern women took factory work during the Civil War.

drew on the efforts of thousands of women in towns and villages throughout the North.

Women also took over the work of men who had gone off to fight. Across the North and South, women took charge of family farms and plantations as their men battled in Antietam or Chancellorsville or Gettysburg—or lay languishing in makeshift army hospitals or military prisons. Some women despaired at the enormous responsibilities of planting, plowing, and running a farm, but other women met the challenge head on—and discovered new strengths and abilities in the process. Sarah Morgan of Baton Rouge, Louisiana, marveled at how much she accomplished in one day—"empty a dirty hearth, dust, move heavy weights, make myself generally useful and dirty, and all this thanks to the Yankees."

Throughout the North, scores of women worked in government offices for the first time to replace male clerks who had enlisted in the Union army. They worked as clerks and copyists, copying speeches and documents for government records. They also became postal employees and worked in the Treasury Department cutting apart long sheets of paper money and counting currency. Salaries ranged from $500 to $900 a year by 1865. Although this was more than what most other female employees made at the time, women still earned half of what men had earned for the same work.

Northern women also worked in factories sewing uniforms. Despite the increased demand for their talents, there were always more seamstresses plying their trade than there was work available for them. Soldiers' wives and widows all sought paid work, and sewing was often the only skill they had.

Even when they did work, seamstresses seldom made enough to support themselves. The amount of work available to sewing women —and the wages they were paid—actually declined during the war. Working 14 to 16 hours, many seamstresses earned only 17 to 24 cents a day. From that, they had to pay for the thread they used and any damaged goods.

Women found a special kind of power—an inner power of pride and accomplishment—through serving as military nurses. Shortly after the war began, Union military officials established the Department of Female Nurses. Dorothea Dix, who had earlier dedicated herself to improving conditions in the nation's insane asylums, became superintendent of this new department. She took on the formidable task of recruiting and training nurses for the Union army.

Dix, who was gravely solemn in appearance and manner, recruited only women who were at least 30 and "plain in appearance." She rejected applicants who were too fashionably dressed or adorned in jewelry. Dix wanted to make sure that her nurses were above reproach in appearance and manner, and that they dedicated themselves to their work. Under Dix's supervision, more than 3,000 female nurses joined the Union effort. They earned a monthly salary of $12.

One job of battlefront nurses was to write letters home for wounded soldiers. Many nurses were dispatched by church groups or missionary societies. Orders of nuns, such as the Sisters of Charity, also volunteered their nursing skills.

But one of the most distinguished Union nurses during the war was not affiliated with Dix's Department of Female Nurses. Instead, Clara Barton sallied forth on her own, working in Union battlefield hospitals and sometimes on the battlefield itself. Barton was a slender, petite woman with a round, open face and a gentle, caring countenance. But this mild exterior concealed an iron will and an abundance of energy. When the war broke out, she collected supplies from soldiers' relief organizations throughout New England and distributed them herself to Union army camps.

Soon she was nursing wounded and dying men as they were brought in from the battlefield. On her own, she learned how to dress wounds, tie a tourniquet around bloodied limbs to stem the

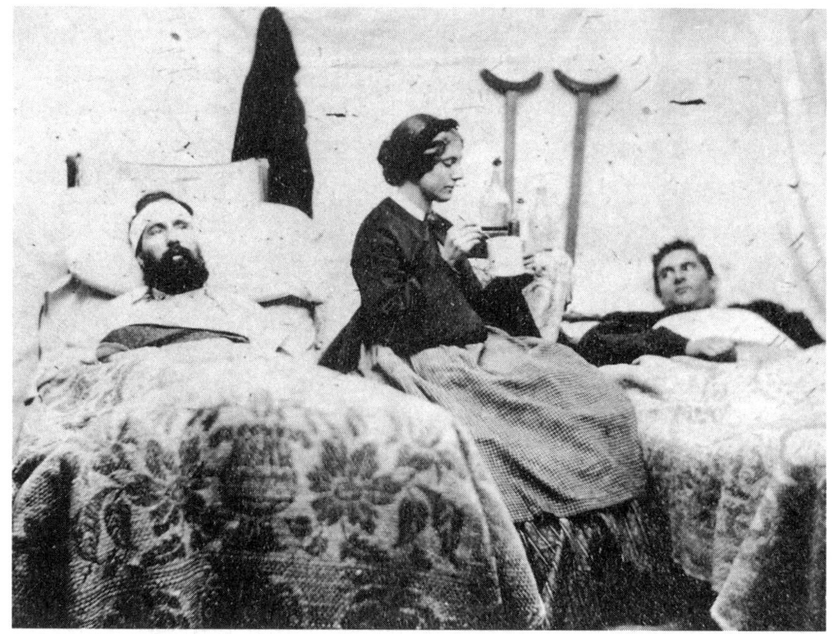

At a Union hospital in Nashville, Tennessee, a nurse feeds a wounded soldier. Nurses were required to be 30 years old and "very plain-looking women. Their dresses must be brown or black, with no bows, no curls, no jewelry and no hoop skirts."

bleeding, and cut a bullet out of human flesh when no doctor was available. Barton called the soldiers "my boys" and ministered to them with a mother's love. She bathed their perspiring faces with wet rags, stroked their hair and read to them, and gave them small dosages of whiskey to ease the pain. Barton herself was never far from the dangers of battle. One day, as she held a wounded soldier in her arms, a bullet whizzed through the sleeve of her dress and killed him.

Sometimes it took all the inner strength that women could muster to perform their nursing tasks. They coped with the tormented screams of men enduring an amputation without the benefit of anesthesia, the ravings of other soldiers delirious from fever and infection, the quiet stoicism of those soldiers who knew they were dying, and the grim reality of death and disease. But nurses and doctors also became accustomed to such overwhelming suffering. Kate Cumming, a Confederate nurse at the Battle of Shiloh in Tennessee, reported in her diary, "The foul air from this mass of human beings at first made me giddy and sick, but I soon got over it. We have to walk, and when we give the men anything kneel, in blood and water; but we think nothing of it at all." After the ferocious battle of Gettysburg, in which 51,000 Union and Confederate soldiers were killed or wounded over three days of fierce fighting, Cornelia Hancock, a volunteer nurse from New Jersey, wrote to her sister, "I feel assured I shall never feel horrified at anything that may happen to me hereafter. . . . I could stand by and see a man's head taken off I believe—you get so used to it here."

Nurses in the Civil War seldom questioned whether they had stepped beyond women's sphere in performing such "indelicate" work. Whether they hailed from the Union or the Confederacy, their patriotic commitment and also their hearts told them they were in the right place during the war.

If some women found their calling as nurses, other women discovered adventure and fulfillment from teaching the former slaves. As the Union armies advanced deeper into the South, capturing Confederate territory and liberating slaves in the process, hundreds of black and white women, mostly in their 20s, followed closely behind to teach the former slaves, many of whom were illiterate. Women risked danger and hardship—and sometimes their families' disapproval—to venture South. They went under the auspices of the American Missionary Society, the Pennsylvania Freedmen's Relief Association, and other agencies that recruited teachers and paid their monthly wages of $10 to $12.

Two slaves work on a grammar lesson with their teacher, Kate Foote, who was sent to South Carolina by the New England Freedman's Aid Society. Teachers set up schools in dreary church basements, former slave pens, and army barracks—wherever they could find enough room and protection from jeering mobs of Southerners who did not want former slaves to receive an education.

Teachers admired their students' eagerness to learn. "It is a great happiness to teach them," Charlotte Forten, a black woman who taught in the Sea Islands off of South Carolina, wrote a friend in November 1862. "I wish some of those persons at the North who say the race is hopelessly and naturally inferior, could see the readiness with which these children, so long oppressed and deprived of every privilege, learn and understand." Adult ex-slaves, too, were willing students. Of one of her grown-up students, Forten remarked, "I never saw anyone so determined to learn."

Nursing and teaching were traditional forms of women's work, performed in the rush and excitement of war. But women also did untraditional work during the war. Both black and white women worked as spies, scouts, and smugglers. Mary Elizabeth Bowser, a former slave, became a servant in the home of Confederate president Jefferson Davis—to relay military information overheard in the Davis household to the Union side.

Two other former slaves, a husband and wife, cleverly devised a system in which the wife, who got herself hired as a laundress for

Captain Sally Tomkins was the only Confederate woman to hold a military commission during the Civil War, though she refused a salary. She was commander of the Robertson Hospital in Richmond, Virginia, where she and her staff of 6 cared for more than 1,300 men.

the family of a southern officer, sent messages via the clothesline to her husband, who worked on the Union side. Each article of clothing that she hung on the line represented a movement of Confederate troops. As her husband explained, "That there gray shirt is [Confederate general James] Longstreet; and when she takes it off, it means he's gone down about Richmond." In general, ex-slaves spied for the North because they wanted to help defeat slavery.

About 400 women disguised themselves as Union or Confederate soldiers and fought in the war. With the proper attire, some could easily pass for being a man. Women enlisted for a variety of reasons—some believed in the cause so deeply that they would not let being a woman stop them from fighting as soldiers. Others craved the adventure or could not bear to be apart from husbands or other loved ones who had joined the army. No doubt some women were killed in battle and went to their graves with their true identities concealed.

Other women soldiers were forced to reveal their secret when they were wounded. A female Union soldier, wounded in the battle of Chickamauga in Tennessee, was captured by Confederate troops and returned to the Union side with a note: "As the Confederates do not use women in the war, this woman, wounded in battle, is returned to you." When a Union nurse asked her why she had joined the army, she replied, "I thought I'd like camp life, and I did."

For the first two years of the war, Confederate forces won most of the major battles. The Union army, even with its superior resources, floundered from one battle to another under a succession of inept Union generals. Finally, on September 18, 1862, the Army of the Potomac achieved its first significant victory—at Antietam Creek in Sharpsburg, Maryland. The cost of victory was enormous. In one day, nearly 6,000 men on both sides were killed and another 17,000 were wounded.

But the victory impelled Lincoln to do something that he had been contemplating for a long time—to issue an Emancipation Proclamation to free southern slaves. On September 22, 1862, he issued a preliminary Emancipation Proclamation. This proclamation warned the Confederate states that all slaves held in any state still in rebellion against the Union on January 1, 1863, would be "thenceforward, and forever free."

With one stroke of the pen, Lincoln had turned the Civil War into a war to abolish slavery as well as to preserve the Union. By giving the war this added moral purpose, he infused new fighting spirit in Union troops, won the support of other nations that condemned slavery, such as Great Britain, and gave southern slaves renewed hope that the "day of jubilee"—freedom—would soon arrive.

But for most slaves, the outward circumstances of their lives changed little. Most of them stayed on their plantations, some journeyed to refugee camps set up by the Union army, and some went in search of family members who had been sold to other plantations. For all slaves, the war brought new hardships and new challenges. On plantations, the work load seemed to double as white men went off to fight and slave men were either forced into service by the Confederate army or recruited by the Union army. Eliza Scantling, who was 15 in 1865, recalled that in the early months of that year, she "plowed a mule an' a wild un at dat. Sometimes me hands get so cold I jes' cry."

When slave fathers joined the Union army, slave mothers and children suffered the wrath of cruel owners. In 1863, one slave woman wrote to her soldier husband: "I have had nothing but trouble since you left . . . they abuse me because you went & say they will not take care of our children & do nothing but quarrel with me all the time and beat me scandalously the day before yesterday."

Despite such ill treatment, or the upheaval of living in refugee camps, or the uncertainties that lay ahead, slaves rejoiced at their emancipation because it meant that their families could be together. Hundreds of black couples began to legalize marriage ties. In slavery, they had married without benefit of a prescribed civil or religious ritual that was legally binding, and planters were free to break up these marriages. Now, as free people, couples yearned to make their marriages legal—and to reunite family members who had been sold among various plantations.

As the war dragged on, African-American and white women on the southern homefront bore the worst hardships, because the war was fought mostly on their soil. As Union forces moved farther south, entire homes, neighborhoods, and towns were destroyed. Almost as difficult to bear were the constant shortages of food and the astro-

Frances Clalin's gaunt features aided her disguise as a private in the 13th Maine Cavalry. On both sides, some 400 women managed to disguise themselves in order to fight, but in the field their true identities were usually discovered.

nomical price of everyday items. The Union blockade of southern ports deprived Southerners of both the necessities and luxuries they had always taken for granted.

Because food was scarce and an unstable Confederate currency continually drove prices higher, basic foodstuffs became unaffordable. People gave up drinking coffee, because the cost of beans had skyrocketed to $70 a pound. Instead, they made do by brewing okra seeds, toasted yams, and roasted corn. In Richmond, a barrel of flour cost as much as $70—beyond the means of most families. By early 1865, bacon and butter in Petersburg, Virginia, cost $20 a pound, and chickens ran as high as $50 apiece.

Worries over how to stretch meager dollars and provisions, and how to protect their homes and possessions from ruin, took a terrible toll on southern women. "I experience such constant dread and anxiety," Lila Chunn wrote her soldier husband, William, in the spring of 1863, "that I feel all the time weary and depressed." One southern woman was so despondent that she felt as if she "could willingly say 'good night' to the world and all in it."

Other southern women aimed their wrath at Union soldiers occupying their cities. In her journal, Eliza Andrews fumed, "If all the words of hatred in every language under heaven were summed up together into one huge epithet of detestation, they could not tell how I hate Yankees. They thwart all my plans, murder my friends, and make my life miserable." In New Orleans, women showed their back sides to Union general Benjamin Butler in public and pasted his picture to the bottom of chamber pots.

Northern women suffered too, though they experienced far less hardship than southern women. Up North, everyday items were also scarce because so many goods were being redirected to the war front. As a result, the cost of living also rose beyond the means of many people. Thousands of soldiers' families went hungry, and women who had never had to ask for charity were mortified that they now had to seek assistance.

In 1863, women in New York City went on a rampage. In the South, women had rioted for food; in New York they joined men, mostly Irish, who were protesting against a federal provision that allowed draftees to hire substitutes. The protest quickly erupted into a riot against the city's blacks. The protesters, who feared competition from black workers, resented being drafted to fight a war for the slave's freedom. Even more so, they resented upper-class Yankee Protestants who could afford to pay substitutes $300 to fight in their places.

Over four days, rioters looted stores and beat innocent blacks. Angry mobs lynched about six blacks, destroyed the dwellings where blacks lived, and burned down the Colored Orphan Asylum. They also set fire to several businesses that employed blacks and destroyed the homes of prominent Republicans and abolitionists. Women took part in the plunder, venting their rage at a government and a war that sacrificed their men and impoverished their lives.

But for all women, North and South, the hardest part of war was losing beloved husbands, sons, and fathers in battle. This cruelty knew no boundaries. Across the battered nation, women feared receiving telegrams with the dreaded news. "A telegram comes to you," Mary Boykin Chesnut wrote, "and you leave it in your lap. You are pale with fright. You handle it, or dread to touch it, as you would a rattlesnake—worse—worse. A snake would only strike you."

Sometimes women found out not from a telegram but from a list published in the newspaper or posted at the train depot. Harriet Beecher Stowe learned that her son Fred had been wounded at Gettysburg from her morning paper. In 1862, an Arkansas woman

Along with a clergyman, Southern women tend the grave of Confederate hero Stonewall Jackson. Southern women showed their devotion to the Confederate cause by organizing memorial associations to maintain the graves of their fallen heroes.

learned the awful news in a more devastating way—by stumbling upon the bodies of her husband and two brothers on the battlefield at Prairie Grove, Arkansas. By the end of the war, almost every American family had lost a dear relative or friend; and thousands of families coped with the formidable task of caring for a loved one maimed in battle.

A religious person might have looked for some higher meaning or purpose in this unfathomable suffering. That is precisely what Lincoln did as he stepped forward on a windy, gloomy March day in 1865 to take the Presidential oath of office once more. "Fondly do we hope," he said, "fervently do we pray—that this mighty scourge of war may speedily pass away. Yet, if God wills that it continue, until all the wealth piled by the bondsman's two hundred and fifty years of unrequited toil shall be sunk, and until every drop of blood drawn with the lash, shall be paid by another drawn with the sword . . . it must be said 'the judgments of the Lord, are true and righteous altogether.'" Then the President appealed for a speedy end to the war and a "just, and a lasting peace, among ourselves, and with all nations."

As the mighty Union forces encircled the battered Confederate army, a speedy end was indeed in sight. On April 9, 1865, Robert E. Lee, commander of what was left of the Confederate forces, surrendered to General Ulysses S. Grant, commanding officer of the Army of the Potomac. While southern women remained closeted in their homes, the window blinds tightly shut as if they were in mourning, a joyous North erupted into celebration. People thronged the streets, laughing, hugging, greeting one another like old friends, and bells merrily pealed atop church steeples.

But this gleeful, noisy spectacle was abruptly silenced by an assassin's bullet. On the evening of April 14, 1865, Good Friday, Lincoln was shot by John Wilkes Booth, a loyal Confederate. The President died quietly the next morning without regaining consciousness, and Northerners mourned their fallen leader.

Mary Chesnut, wife of the first Southern senator to resign from the U.S. Senate, kept a journal throughout the Civil War. Her keen observations offered a revealing glimpse into the hardships endured by Southern women during the war.

Women in both the North and South anxiously awaited the return of their menfolk from the battlefields and tried to put their own lives back in order. For Southerners, the immediate task was to repair their shattered homes and cities and eke out a living. Most of the South had been reduced to rubble. Mail service, police protection, bridges, roads, and public buildings—all were in disarray. Local and state governments were in chaos, and the Confederate currency was worthless.

But the North, while mostly untouched by the physical devastation of war, shared in the shocking number of casualties. No war before or since has cost so many American lives. More than 600,000 soldiers were killed—more than one out of every five soldiers nationwide. Countless others were crippled for life.

As women across the nation reflected upon the last four years of Civil War, upon all the sacrifices and hardships, perhaps they took pride in the vital roles they had played during the war. Now it was time to set their sights on the future. Slavery had been abolished and all African Americans were legally free. But the battle for a "new birth of freedom," as Lincoln had eloquently declared at Gettysburg, was not yet finished—certainly not for America's women. They had yet to achieve the fruits of victory in their struggle for political, economic, and social equality. The coming years would be busy ones indeed, as American women labored to extend the democratic ideals and hopes nobly expressed during the war to their own lives.

ISAAC and ROSA, Emancipated Slave Children,
From the Free Schools of Louisiana,
Photographed by KIMBALL, 477 Broadway. N.Y.
Entered according to Act of Congress, in the year 1863 by GEO. H. HANKS. in the Clerk's Office of the U. S. for the Sou. Dist. of N.Y.

"WE'SE FREE NOW"

In a Memorial Day address in 1888, almost a quarter of a century after the Civil War, Clara Barton told a Boston audience that when the war ended, "woman was at least fifty years in advance of the normal position which continued peace . . . would have assigned her." Barton may have been exaggerating, but the Civil War surely did create new opportunities for women. The war hastened women's entry into nursing and teaching, and eventually elevated both occupations into highly respectable professions. In addition, women found more employment opportunities in factories, offices, and department stores—although in the immediate aftermath of war, some women had to give up their jobs to returning soldiers.

Perhaps more importantly, many women discovered new strengths and abilities from their war work. This expansive self-confidence stayed with them as they rebuilt their lives out of the wreckage of war. Clara Barton went on to found the American Red Cross and to serve her country once more as a nurse in the Spanish-American War. Elizabeth Cady Stanton, Susan B. Anthony, and other women's rights activists renewed their crusade for women's social and political equality, fully confident that the nation would grant women suffrage and other rights. Though a long struggle lay ahead of them, they used new organizing techniques and ideas acquired through their war work to press forward.

Freed from slavery in 1863, these children bear enormous dignity as they stroll into a life of freedom.

Clara Barton, self-trained as a nurse during the Civil War, went on to found the American Red Cross.

But perhaps some of the biggest success stories took place in the South, where women literally had to sift through the rubble of former homes to piece their lives back together. Ella Gertrude Thomas of Georgia is one such success story. During the postwar years, she became the main breadwinner in her family. As her husband sank into despair and gambled away the family's small savings in bad investments, Thomas took up teaching and wrote a newspaper column.

While her husband's health and hopes ebbed and their savings dwindled, she marshaled new inner resources to keep the family going. "I think and think boldly," she wrote in her journal. "I act—and act boldly." In later years, she joined the Woman's Christian Temperance Union; worked for prison and educational reform; and served as president of the Georgia Woman Suffrage Association. She spoke out against wife abuse and discrimination against women, and insisted upon women's right to vote and take control of their lives.

Thomas's transformation from a high-society antebellum mistress to a dedicated political activist was remarkable—perhaps she would have traveled this path anyway without the fiery trial of Civil War. But she was one of many southern women who turned misfortune to her benefit, developed new strengths and overcame adversity—and, in the process, punctured the antebellum image of the frail, helpless southern belle, an image once used to justify southern men's power over white women of all classes.

In freedom, African-American women endured many of the hardships they had known in slavery. They lived meager, impoverished lives and worked from dawn to dusk—often as field workers for former masters. Many suffered brutal physical abuse by whites who thought nothing of treating free human beings as though they were still slaves—although the 13th Amendment to the Constitution, ratified on December 6, 1865, outlawed slavery once and for all in the United States. Southern blacks were plagued by the petty humiliations as well as the ruthless terror visited upon them by whites who wanted to keep all blacks socially and politically powerless.

But black women and men of the postwar South knew they were no longer enslaved, and they exercised their right to live as free human beings. At the end of the war, a freedwoman who had been separated from her young daughter in slavery came to the "big house" to retrieve her. Her former mistress begged, "Let her stay with me." But the woman knew her rights. She shook her head and replied, "You took her away from me an' didn' pay no mind to my cryin', so now I'se takin' her back home. We'se free now, Mis' Polly, we ain't gwine be slaves no more to nobody."

During the Civil War, Mary Bowser worked as a household servant for Elizabeth Van Lew in Richmond, Virginia. Both women were Union spies. By 1900, when this photograph was taken, Bowser had become a prosperous citizen of nearby Petersburg.

CHRONOLOGY

1848	The United States acquires California, Arizona, Nevada, Utah, and parts of Colorado and New Mexico after winning the Mexican War; gold discovered in California Married Woman's Property Act passed in New York State; grants married women ownership over property inherited or acquired
July 19-20, 1848	First women's rights convention in U.S. at Seneca Falls, New York
August 1848	Second women's rights convention in Rochester, New York; first time a woman chairs a meeting
1849	Amelia Bloomer establishes the *Lily,* a temperance journal; soon shifts focus to women's rights
1850	Congress passes Compromise of 1850, enacts stronger fugitive slave law Female Medical College of Pennsylvania, first medical school for women, established
October 23, 1850	First national women's rights convention in Worcester, Massachusetts; delegates decide to circulate petitions for woman suffrage
1852	Harriet Beecher Stowe publishes *Uncle Tom's Cabin*
1853	Paulina Wright Davis establishes *Una,* one of the first women's rights journals
1857	U.S. Supreme Court rules in *Dred Scott* case that a slave is not a citizen and reinforces planters' property rights over slaves
1860	Abraham Lincoln elected U.S. President
February 9, 1861	Jefferson Davis elected president of Confederate States of America
April 12, 1861	Civil War begins
January 1, 1863	Lincoln issues final Emancipation Proclamation; liberates African-American slaves in all Confederate states still in rebellion
April 9, 1865	Civil War ends
April 14, 1865	John Wilkes Booth assassinates Lincoln
December 6, 1865	13th Amendment to the U.S. Constitution is ratified; outlaws slavery

FURTHER READING

A Note on Sources

In the interest of readability, the volumes in this series include no discussion of historiography and no footnotes. As works of synthesis and overview, however, they are greatly indebted to the research and writing of other historians. The principal works drawn on in this volume are among the books listed below.

General Histories of Women

Blumenthal, Shirley, and Jerome S. Ozer, eds. *Coming to America: Immigrants from the British Isles.* New York: Delacorte, 1980.

Chambers-Schiller, Lee Virginia. *Liberty: A Better Husband.* New Haven, Conn.: Yale University Press, 1984.

Evans, Sarah M. *Born for Liberty: A History of Women in America.* New York: Free Press, 1989.

Jones, Jacqueline. *Labor of Love, Labor of Sorrow: Black Women, Work, and the Family from Slavery to the Present.* New York: Basic Books, 1985.

Kessler-Harris, Alice. *Out to Work.* New York: Oxford University Press, 1982.

Lerner, Gerda, ed. *Black Women in White America.* New York: Vintage, 1973.

Solomon, Barbara. *In the Company of Educated Women: A History of Women and Higher Education in America.* New Haven, Conn.: Yale University Press, 1985.

Sterling, Dorothy, ed. *We Are Your Sisters.* New York: Norton, 1984.

Weatherford, Doris. *Foreign & Female: Immigrant Women in America, 1840–1930.* New York: Schocken, 1986.

Weiner, Lynn. *From Working Girl to Working Mother: The Female Labor Force in the United States, 1820–1980.* Chapel Hill: University of North Carolina Press, 1985.

Wertheimer, Barbara Mayer. *We Were There: The Story of Working Women in America.* New York: Pantheon, 1977.

19th-Century History

Alcott, Louisa May. *Hospital Sketches.* New York: Sagamore Press, 1957.

Ames, Mary. *From a New England Woman's Diary in Dixie in 1865.* New York: Negro Universities Press, 1969.

Anderson, John Q., ed. *Brokenburn: The Journal of Kate Stone, 1861–1868.* Baton Rouge: Louisiana State University Press, 1972.

Berlin, Ira, et al., eds. *Free at Last: A Documentary History of Slavery, Freedom, and the Civil War.* New York: New Press, 1992.

Bleser, Carol, ed. *In Joy and in Sorrow: Women, Family, and Marriage in the Victorian South, 1830–1900.* New York: Oxford University Press, 1991.

Braude, Ann. *Radical Spirits: Spiritualism and Women's Rights in Nineteenth-Century America.* Boston: Beacon, 1992.

Chang, Ina. *A Separate Battle: Women and the Civil War.* New York: Lodestar Books, 1991.

Clinton, Catherine. *The Other Civil War: American Women in the Nineteenth Century.* New York: Hill and Wang, 1984.

———. *The Plantation Mistress: Woman's World in the Old South.* New York: Pantheon, 1982.

Clinton, Catherine, and Nina Silber, eds. *Divided Houses: Gender and the Civil War.* New York: Oxford University Press, 1992.

Diner, Hasia R. *Erin's Daughters in America: Irish Immigrant Women in the Nineteenth Century.* Baltimore: Johns Hopkins University Press, 1983.

Dublin, Thomas. *Farm to Factory: Women's Letters, 1830–1860.* New York: Columbia University Press, 1981.

Faragher, John Mack. *Women and Men on the Overland Trail.* New Haven, Conn.: Yale University Press, 1979.

Fox-Genovese, Elizabeth. *Within the Plantation Household: Black and White Women of the Old South.* Chapel Hill: University of North Carolina Press, 1988.

Franklin, John Hope. *From Slavery to Freedom.* 5th ed. New York: Knopf, 1988.

Hersh, Blanche Glassman. *The Slavery of Sex: Feminist Abolitionists in America.* Urbana: University of Illinois Press, 1978.

Massey, Mary Elizabeth. *Bonnet Brigades.* New York: Knopf, 1966.

McPherson, James M. *Battle Cry of Freedom: The Civil War Era.* New York: Oxford University Press, 1988.

Meltzer, Milton, ed. *Voices from the Civil War.* New York: Crowell, 1989.

Mohrs, James C., ed. *The Cormany Diaries: A Northern Family in the Civil War.* Pittsburgh: University of Pittsburgh Press, 1982.

Myres, Sandra L. *Westering Women and the Frontier Experience: 1800–1915.* Albuquerque: University of New Mexico Press, 1982.

Scott, Anne Firor. *The Southern Lady.* Chicago: University of Chicago Press, 1970.

White, Deborah Gray. *Ar'n't I a Woman?: Female Slaves in the Plantation South.* New York: Norton, 1985.

Biographies

Bacon, Margaret Hope. *Valiant Friend: The Life of Lucretia Mott.* New York: Walker, 1980.

Banner, Lois W. *Elizabeth Cady Stanton: A Radical for Woman's Rights.* Boston: Little, Brown, 1980.

Cooper, Ilene. *Susan B. Anthony.* New York: Franklin Watts, 1984.

Ortiz, Victoria. *Sojourner Truth: A Self-Made Woman.* Philadelphia: Lippincott, 1974.

Pryor, Elizabeth Brown. *Clara Barton: Professional Angel.* Philadelphia: University of Pennsylvania Press, 1987.

Sklar, Kathyrn Kish. *Catharine Beecher: A Study in American Domesticity.* New Haven, Conn.: Yale University Press, 1973.

Woodward, C. Vann, ed. *Mary Chesnut's Civil War.* New Haven, Conn.: Yale University Press, 1981.

Woodward, C. Vann, and Elisabeth Muhlenfeld, eds. *The Private Mary Chesnut: The Unpublished Civil War Diaries.* New York: Oxford University Press, 1984.

INDEX

References to illustrations are indicated by page numbers in *italics*.

Acknowledgments

I am grateful to Professor Nancy F. Cott, general editor of this series, who gave me the opportunity to write this volume. Her sensitive reading of the manuscript and her astute comments and suggestions greatly improved the book. Nancy Toff, executive editor at Oxford University Press, has been a pleasure to work with. Whether she was cheerfully snipping away at extraneous material or polishing jagged prose, she has been thoroughly professional and cooperative. Along with Professor Cott, she contributed immensely to refining the manuscript. I also extend my thanks to Tara Deal, project editor, and Paul McCarthy, assistant project editor, both at Oxford, for shepherding the manuscript through its many stages to a finished book.

Professor Stephen B. Oates, Paul Murray Kendall Professor of Biography at the University of Massachusetts at Amherst, kindly lent me his current work on Clara Barton. He first stimulated my interest in women's roles during the Civil War, and his passionate commitment to artful historical writing has inspired me immeasurably.

Finally, a special thanks to three people: my father, Leon Sigerman, and my stepmother, Marilyn Sigerman, for their abiding interest and encouragement; and Jay, whose love and enthusiasm for this project sustained me through the months of research and writing.

Picture Credits

Abby Aldrich Rockefeller Folk Art Center: 72; American Red Cross: 134; Amistad Research Center, New Orleans, Louisiana: 22; Archives of Industrial Society, Hillman Library, University of Pittsburgh: 97; Courtesy the Bancroft Library, University of California, Berkeley: 69; The Bettmann Archive: 100; Boston Atheneum: 29, 45, 92, 95; Courtesy of the Bostonian Society, Old State House: 41; California State Library, California Section: 51, 64, 66, 70, 73; Cincinnati Historical Society: 37, 39, 71; The Connecticut Historical Society, Hartford: 58; Duke University, Special Collections Library: 119-R; John A. Hess: 114, 128-L, 128-R; Courtesy The Historic New Orleans Collection, Museum/Research Center: 18 (Acc. Nos. 1975.93.1 and 1975.93.2), 24 (Acc. No. 1965.871, ii); Historical Society of Pennsylvania: 23; Library of Congress: cover, 10, 13, 14, 16, 20-T, 25, 27, 28, 30, 31, 32, 35, 38, 55, 56, 57, 60, 61, 62, 63, 67, 78, 80, 109, 110, 119-L, 122, 132; Courtesy of the Louisiana State Museum: 20-B; Lowell National Historic Park: 105, 106; Lynn Historical Society, Lynn, Mass.: 101, 111; Minnesota Historical Society: 75; Mount Holyoke College Library/Archives: 85; Museum of American Textile History: 98, 102, 103, 104, 112; Museum of the City of New York, *The Bay & Harbor of New York,* 1847, by Samuel B. Waugh. Gift of Mrs. Robert M. Littlejohn: 77; Museum of the City of New York, *Women's Central Relief Association At Cooper Union,* 1865. Gift of Mrs. J. West Roosevelt: 121; National Portrait Gallery, Smithsonian Institution: 131; Nebraska State Historical Society: 7; Collection of The New-York Historical Society: 59, 93; North Carolina Collection, University of North Carolina Library, Chapel Hill: 88; Oberlin College Archives: 46, 82, 86, 87; Ohio Historical Society: 15; Collection of the Onondaga Historical Association, Syracuse, New York: 21; Courtesy of the Archives of the Pennsylvania Academy of Fine Arts, Philadelphia: 117; Schlesinger Library, Radcliffe College: 89, 90, 96; Schomburg Center for Research in Black Culture, New York Public Library, Astor, Lenox and Tilden Foundations: 12-T, 12-B, 52; Smithsonian Institution: 54, 84; Society of California Pioneers: 74; Sophia Smith Collection, Smith College, Northampton, Mass.: 48; South Caroliniana Library, University of South Carolina: 120; The Stowe-Day Foundation, Hartford, Conn.: 94, 125; Swarthmore College, Friends Historical Library: 34, 40, 44; U.S. Army Military History Institute, Carlisle, Pennsylvania: 123, 124; University of Rochester Library, Department of Rare Books and Special Collections: 36, 43; Valentine Museum, Richmond, Virginia: 19, 126, 135; Virginia Military Institute Archives: 130; Virginia State Library and Archives: 116, 118; The Western Reserve Historical Society, Cleveland, Ohio: frontispiece; Worcester Historical Museum: 47.

Harriet Sigerman is a historian and freelance writer who has contributed to *European Immigrant Women in the United States: A Biographical Dictionary* and *The Young Reader's Companion to American History*. She has been a research assistant to Henry Steele Commager at Amherst College and for the Stanton-Anthony Papers at the University of Massachusetts at Amherst. A graduate of the University of California at Irvine, she holds an M.A. and Ph.D. in American history from the University of Massachusetts at Amherst.

Nancy F. Cott is Stanley Woodward Professor of history and American studies at Yale University. She is the author of *The Bonds of Womanhood: "Woman's Sphere" in New England 1780–1835*, *The Grounding of Modern Feminism*, and *A Woman Making History: Mary Ritter Beard Through Her Letters;* editor of *Root of Bitterness: Documents of the Social History of American Women;* and co-editor of *A Heritage of Her Own: Toward a New Social History of American Women.*